COLLINS LIVING HISTORY

Medieval realms
1066-1500

Christopher Culpin
Series editor: Christopher Culpin

CollinsEducational
An imprint of HarperCollins*Publishers*

Contents

attainment target 1

Questions aimed at this attainment target find out how much you know and understand about the past. Some questions are about how things were different in history: not only people's food, or clothes but their beliefs too. Others are about how things change through history, sometimes quickly, sometimes slowly, sometimes a little, sometimes a lot. Other questions ask you to explain why things were different in the past, and why changes took place.

attainment target 2

This attainment target is about understanding what people say about the past. Historians, as well as lots of other people, try to describe what the past was like. Sometimes they say different things. This attainment target is about understanding these differences and why they occur.

attainment target 3

This attainment target is about historical sources and how we use them to find out about the past. Some questions are about the historical evidence we can get from sources. Others ask you about how valuable this evidence might be.

Introduction

The past is like a foreign country: people did the same things that we do, but they did them differently. For example, the picture below shows a busy port in England in the 15th century. There are ships bringing goods from abroad, there is evidence of inland transport – a pack horse, two pubs – the buildings in the bottom corners and there is a crowded town in the background.

In this book we will look at how people lived in Britain in medieval times. We will find out about ordinary men, women and children, about what they believed, how they were governed and about the big and small events in their lives. We will see how their lives were different from ours, and sometimes how they were the same.

People find out about the past by using sources of evidence. This book is full of sources of all kinds for you to learn from such as pictures, like this one, letters, poems, official documents and photographs of objects and buildings.

William's invasion

The Bayeux tapestry

The Bayeux tapestry is a piece of needlework, 50 cm wide and 75 metres long. If you look closely at Sources 1 and 2 you can see the stitches the needlewomen made. They used eight colours of wool, all made from natural dyes. Can you find all eight colours?

The tapestry tells the story of how William, Duke of Normandy, invaded England and defeated King Harold of England at the battle of Hastings (see Source 3). It was made soon after the battle of Hastings took place. It is therefore a primary source of evidence. It is amazing that this fragile piece of cloth has survived when so many things from that time have been lost or destroyed.

Historians need to know how accurate a source is if they are going to use it to find out about the past. The Bayeux tapestry tells the story from the Norman point of view. It was probably made on the orders of Odo, Bishop of Bayeux, and was designed by a Norman (see Source 4). However, the needlewomen may well have been English.

AIMS

In this unit we will find out more about the Norman INVASION **and the Norman** CONQUEST**. We will find out why William invaded England and why Harold clashed with him in battle at Hastings. This unit examines their motives. We will look at sources from both the Norman and the English side. Most importantly, we will find out why 1066 is regarded as one of the most important years in British history.**

SOURCE 1

Duke William of Normandy with his two half-brothers, Odo and Robert, taken from the Bayeux tapestry.

SOURCE 2

Part of the Bayeux tapestry, showing boats carrying the Norman army to invade England.

SOURCE 3
This description of the battle of Hastings is taken from the *Anglo-Saxon Chronicle* for the year 1066.

1 Make a list of the things the Bayeux tapestry does *not* show accurately, for example: size of buildings.

2 Make a list of the things the Bayeux tapestry might show accurately, for example: clothes.

3 On whose side do you think the author of Source 3 was?

4 How can you tell from Source 4 that Bishop Odo was a churchman? Do you think Source 4 is an accurate portrait of him?

5 Compare the trees in Source 4 with the carving in Source 5. Do these sources suggest that the people who stitched the tapestry were English? Give reasons for your answer.

SOURCE 4
Part of the Bayeux tapestry. It shows Bishop Odo giving the order to cut down trees to build ships for the invasion.

SOURCE 5
An English ivory comb from the 11th century.

The old king dies: what next?

It was Christmas, 1065. Edward, King of England, lay dying in London (see Source 6). The death of King Edward would put England at a dangerous crossroads: who would lead the country? And in which direction? Look at Source 7. It shows that there were two powerful forces in North-west Europe at that time: the Vikings and the Normans. Both were a threat to England.

SOURCE 6

The death of Edward the Confessor, from the Bayeux tapestry.

SOURCE 7

North-west Europe in 1065.

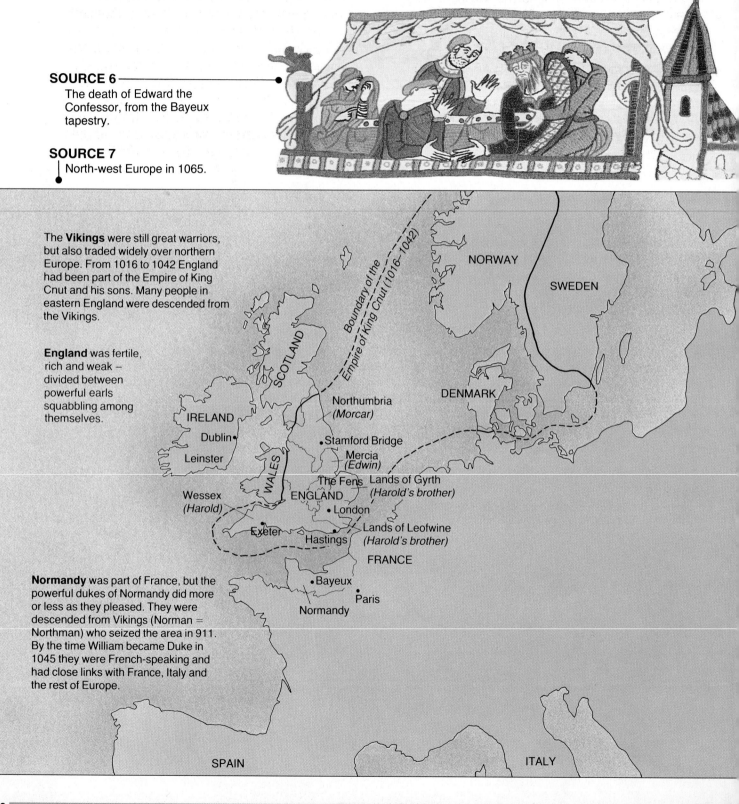

The **Vikings** were still great warriors, but also traded widely over northern Europe. From 1016 to 1042 England had been part of the Empire of King Cnut and his sons. Many people in eastern England were descended from the Vikings.

England was fertile, rich and weak – divided between powerful earls squabbling among themselves.

Normandy was part of France, but the powerful dukes of Normandy did more or less as they pleased. They were descended from Vikings (Norman = Northman) who seized the area in 911. By the time William became Duke in 1045 they were French-speaking and had close links with France, Italy and the rest of Europe.

NORWAY

SWEDEN

Boundary of the Empire of King Cnut (1016–1042)

DENMARK

SCOTLAND

IRELAND

Dublin

Leinster

WALES

Northumbria (Morcar)

Stamford Bridge

Mercia (Edwin)

The Fens   Lands of Gyrth (Harold's brother)

ENGLAND

Wessex (Harold)

London

Exeter

Hastings

Lands of Leofwine (Harold's brother)

FRANCE

Bayeux

Paris

Normandy

SPAIN

ITALY

Edward the Confessor

Edward had failed to deal with this leadership problem while he was king. When Cnut became King of England, the young Edward had been sent by his mother, Emma, to live with her family in Normandy. Edward liked the Normans and lived most of his life as a Norman monk. This continued when he became King of England in 1042. He brought Norman priests and secretaries over to England. He also appointed a Norman to be Bishop of London. Edward spent so much time with his Norman chaplain, confessing his sins, that he was called *Edward the Confessor*. He was married, but he had no children.

For most of his reign, Edward had had to deal with one family that was much more powerful than any other – the family of Godwin, Earl of Wessex. In 1051 Edward had forced Earl Godwin out of England. During the following year Edward promoted more Normans in England; one, Ralph, became Earl of Hereford. Then, in 1052, Godwin forced his way back, and made Edward remove many of his Norman friends from power. When Godwin died in 1053 his son Harold took over the family lands. As Source 7 shows, Harold controlled most of England. He had fought successful wars against Wales, and even against his brother, Tosti, in Northumbria.

ACTIVITY

Under Anglo-Saxon rule, all important decisions in England were taken at a council which was made up of the most important men in the land. This council was called the WITAN.

Work in groups of four to six. You are in London at Christmas 1065. Your group forms the leading members of the Witan. One of the biggest decisions the Witan has ever had to take is who to make king when the old king dies. Think about the factors and the four candidates. Then give your decision, and your reasons. Compare your findings with other groups in the class.

Factors

- The decision as to who should be king lies with the Witan.
- You have to think about members of the Royal Family first, but you do not have to give the crown to one of them.
- You want England to be at peace.
- It looks as if several people might try to take the crown by force.

Candidate	Reasons for	Reasons against
1 Edgar		
2 Harald Hardraada		
3 William		
4 Harold		

Candidates

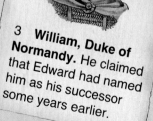

1 **Edward's nearest surviving relative, his nephew Edgar.** He was a boy of 14.

2 **Harald Hardraada.** He was a leading Danish warrior and claimed the throne as Cnut's successor.

3 **William, Duke of Normandy.** He claimed that Edward had named him as his successor some years earlier.

4 **Harold**, son of Earl Godwin.

Make your decision, then copy and fill in the table.

The reign of King Harold

Early in January 1066, Edward the Confessor died. The next day Harold was crowned King of England. Sources 8 to 11 describe this event.

The *Anglo-Saxon Chronicle* is an account of the history of England, which starts at about AD 890. It may have been started on the orders of King Alfred. Several different English monasteries kept their own versions of the Chronicle. Source 9 shows a modern translation of the entry for 1066. Source 10 also describes what happened.

SOURCE 8

Page from the *Anglo-Saxon Chronicle*.

> In this year 1066 King Edward passed away. But the wise King entrusted the kingdom to a great noble – Harold himself. The noble earl always loyally obeyed the King, in words and deeds. Harold was CONSECRATED king, but he did not have a peaceful reign.

SOURCE 9

The *Anglo-Saxon Chronicle* for 1066 describes the death of King Edward.

SOURCE 10

William of Poitiers, William's personal priest, describes how Harold become king.

SOURCE 11

The coronation of Harold, from the Bayeux tapestry.

'Soon there came the bad news that England had lost its king and Harold had been crowned. This hard-hearted Englishman did not wait for the English to acclaim him as king. No, he gathered together a gang of his evil supporters and seized the throne. This was on the day of Edward's funeral, when all the people were very sad at their loss. He was ORDAINED by Stigand, a priest who the pope had EXCOMMUNICATED. So this ceremony did not receive God's blessing.'

RVNT:HAROLDO: NA: REGIS hIC RE REX:AN SIDET:HAROLD GLORVM: STIGANT ARCHIEPS

1 Copy and complete this table.

	Source 9	Source 10
a What the author of this source thinks of Harold		
b Examples to show this		
c Facts you know to be true		
d Facts you know to be false		

2 What would you need to know about the author of Source 9 in order to decide how reliable the source is?

3 Which of Sources 9, 10 and 11 do you think is the most valuable for someone who is studying the events of 1066? Why?

SOURCE 12
Part of the Bayeux tapestry, showing Harold on the throne when he is greeted by a messenger.

The story of the battles of 1066

In the Middle Ages the usual time for war was in the summer. As spring came, Harold had to face his enemies from across the seas. Source 12 shows one of the most remarkable scenes from the Bayeux tapestry. Harold is on the throne when a messenger comes to him. What does the messenger say? The possible answers are in the tapestry borders. In the top border is a star, in fact a comet. This was Halley's Comet, which was visible in England in April 1066. Comets were regarded as signs that unusual events were about to happen. In the bottom border the designer has suggested what these events might be: ghostly invasion ships. Perhaps the messenger is telling Harold that his enemies were planning to invade England.

William of Normandy

One of Harold's rivals was William, Duke of Normandy. William's father, Duke Robert, had died in 1035 when William was only eight. William had faced many dangers before he gained control of Normandy (Source 13).

1 What does Source 13 tell us about life in Normandy?

2 What does Source 13 tell us about William's character?

William grew up to be a tough, determined man, and a skilled soldier. He claimed that Edward had named him to be the next King of England. When William heard that Harold had become king after Edward, he prepared to attack England. As an island, Britain was much more difficult to attack than a country with a land border. William had to build a fleet of ships. Over the centuries since 1066 other people have prepared to invade England by sea. William's fleet was the last to manage this successfully. William also made other preparations: he put together an army. Normandy is quite small, so he called on soldiers from other places as well, and offered them land in England if they won. A force of about 5,000 men (Normans and others) gathered together.

'Often, for fear of my relations, I was smuggled secretly out of the castle at night by my uncle Walter. He took me to the cottages of the poor to save me from discovery by traitors who sought my death.'

SOURCE 13
William describes his childhood in 1035.

The Norman Conquest

How did William, and his 5,000 followers, take over the whole of England? The English did not give up without a fight. In 1067 there was a rebellion in Kent, and in 1068 a more serious one in Exeter, led by Harold's mother. Both rebellions were crushed. Then in 1068 to 1069 Edgar and the remaining English leaders rose in rebellion, helped by the Scots and King Swein of Denmark. William defeated them all, mainly by destroying everything so that the rebels could not find food or shelter. This was called the 'harrying of the north', and left much of northern England devastated for over a century. The last English rebels took refuge in Ely, in the swampy Fens. Here they survived, under their leader, Hereward the Wake, until they were finally crushed in 1071.

Building of castles

William and his followers gained control of the rest of England by building castles. There were very few castles in England before 1066; within a few years there were hundreds. Nearly all these early castles were MOTTE and BAILEY castles. That is, they had a mound, with a wooden stockade around it (the motte) and a larger enclosure (the bailey) as shown in Sources 21 and 22. The Normans forced English workers to build these castles very quickly. From this safe base small groups of Norman knights could ride out to deal with any trouble from the English.

SOURCE 21

Digging a motte and bailey castle. William had this castle built at Hastings in the two weeks between his landing at Pevensey and the battle of Hastings.

SOURCE 22

Reconstruction of a motte and bailey castle at Totnes, Devon.

Other changes

1   William rewarded the knights who had come to fight with him at Hastings by giving them land in England. He removed almost all English landowners and replaced them with his own men.
2   Most English bishops were removed and replaced by Norman bishops.
3   Many fine churches and cathedrals, as well as castles, were built (see Source 23).
4   Norman-French, instead of English, became the language used for all important business.
5   Trade with Normandy and France increased; trade with Scandinavia decreased, especially after the 'harrying of the north'.
6   Many of the laws of England remained the same as they had been in Edward the Confessor's time.

SOURCE 23
Durham Cathedral.

What was William like?

Let us see what people at the time thought about William the Conqueror.

'King William was a very stern and violent man. No one dared do anything against the King's will. He put nobles who annoyed him into prison. He built castles and cruelly kept the poor people down.'

SOURCE 24
A comment on William's character, taken from the *Anglo-Saxon Chronicle*.

'During William's reign the great cathedral at Canterbury was built. Any man was allowed to become a monk, no matter how rich or poor he was. We mustn't forget the good order he kept in the land.'

SOURCE 25
This entry in the *Peterborough Chronicle* describes William's reign.

'Never did William show such cruelty. He did not trouble to restrain his resentment, striking down innocent and guilty alike with an equal fury. In this manner all the sources of life north of the Humber were destroyed.'

SOURCE 26
Orderic Vitalis, usually an admirer of William, wrote this about the 'harrying of the North' in the 12th century.

attainment target 1

1 Draw a time line for the twelve months from Christmas 1065 to Christmas 1066. Mark on it all the events mentioned in this unit.

2 Draw another time line for the years 1064 to 1071. Mark on it all the events mentioned in this unit.

3 Which of the changes in the list do you think happened quickly, and which happened slowly? What did not change?

4 Which of the changes in the list would affect an ordinary English man or woman the most?

Did Harold get shot in the eye?

Source 18 shows the death of Harold, with an arrow in his eye. However, some historians have argued that Harold is the man falling down at the far right of the picture, with no arrow. Nor is this arrow mentioned by the chronicles (see Source 19). Not only is this an interesting argument, but an important one. At this time blinding was a mark of disgrace, of God's anger with you. Recently people have looked closely at the figure lying down: at the back of the tapestry small holes can be seen next to this man's eye. Clearly there was once an arrow stitched in here. It seems that this man is meant to be Harold, blinded and disgraced in his death.

1 What different views of William are given in Sources 24 to 26?

2 What impression of William do you get from reading about him in this unit?

3 Explain why there are these different views of William.

4 What is your own opinion of William's character and personality?

The power of the monarch

AIMS

In this unit we will find out how England's monarchs ran the country in the Middle Ages. We will learn what they could do and what they were not allowed to do. The GOVERNMENT of the country was based on the FEUDAL SYSTEM. This unit will explain what this meant and how it could sometimes go wrong.

We will also see how a monarch's personality becomes very important if he or she makes all the major decisions for the government of the country. We will look at different opinions of the personalities of medieval monarchs, held by writers from this period and by modern historians.

Who controls Britain? Source 1 shows Queen Elizabeth II and the Prime Minister. The Prime Minister is the leader of the political party that has the largest number of Members of Parliament in the HOUSE OF COMMONS. It is the Prime Minister, with the help of other ministers, who runs Britain. The Queen has to agree to all the laws that the Prime Minister and Parliament want to pass. Each year at the State Opening of Parliament, the Queen gives a speech in which she explains what Parliament will be doing during the following year. But it is the Prime Minister who writes the speech.

However, in 1066, when William I became King of England, there was no Parliament, no House of Commons and no Prime Minister. It was the MONARCH who ruled the country. Throughout the MIDDLE AGES England was a monarchy, ruled mostly by kings (see Sources 2 and 3).

In September 1066, when William left France to invade England, his title was duke of Normandy. When he defeated Harold at the battle of Hastings he made himself King of England. The type of monarchy that he built up formed the pattern for other English monarchs for the rest of the Middle Ages.

SOURCE 1

The Queen, Elizabeth II, and the Prime Minister, Mr John Major.

SOURCE 2 ————————————●
Tomb of Henry III.

'The king was taller than most people and was well-built and handsome. He was very athletic and could equal or beat anyone else in most sports. He had excellent manners and could understand all the languages used in the countries between France and the Holy Land, but was fluent only in French and Latin. He was good at law-making and organising the government and he could get at the truth in difficult law cases.

He didn't mind the discomforts of travelling, dust and mud. He was always on the move, and he travelled unbearable distances each day. His court had to struggle after him as well as it could. Henry II was a great expert on hounds and hawks and loved the foolish sport of hunting. He worked all the time and never seemed to sleep.'

SOURCE 3
A description of King Henry II by Walter Map, a priest who knew him well.

1 What did you learn about the personality of William I from Unit 1?

2 What does Source 3 tell you about the personality of Henry II?

3 What are the similarities and differences in your answers to questions 1 and 2?

4 Which qualities did a medieval king or queen need that a modern Prime Minister and queen *do not* need?

5 Which qualities does a modern Prime Minister need that a medieval monarch did *not* need?

6 Look at Source 2. What type of personality do you think Henry III had?

7 Why was the personality of the monarch so important in the Middle Ages?

The feudal system

In the Middle Ages land was the root of all power. The more land you owned the more powerful you became. After the battle of Hastings, William rewarded his followers by giving them land in England. Source 4 shows that William gave his barons large amounts of land. He also gave land to the Church because the pope had supported his invasion of England. In return for this support, William reorganised the Church in England. To do this he appointed NORMANS as bishops and abbots as you can see in Source 5.

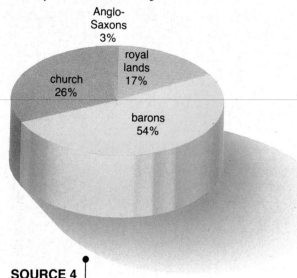

Anglo-Saxons 3%

royal lands 17%

church 26%

barons 54%

SOURCE 4
Pie chart to show William's land grants.

How far does Source 4 support the opinions of the author of Source 5?

SOURCE 6 ────────────────

The feudal system.

'England has become the dwelling-place of foreigners, and is owned by aliens. At the present time there is no English earl, or bishop, or abbot. They are all strangers and they feed upon the riches and the body of England.'

SOURCE 5
From the chonicle of a monk, William of Malmesbury, in 1125.

Source 4 shows that William of Malmesbury in Source 5 was right: the English had their land taken from them and given to Norman barons.

However, William did not give away 83% of England. He said that he owned all the land and was lending it to his followers in return for something. A piece of land lent in this way was called a FEUDUM, so William's system became known as the feudal system.

In Source 6 you can see how the feudal system works. On the right it shows the king giving land to one of his barons. The baron points to the land, which now belongs to him, and clasps hands with the king. He swears an oath that the king will be his OVERLORD and he will be the king's VASSAL (servant). This is called the oath of HOMAGE (see Source 7).

In return for the land William had the service of a certain number of soldiers at the baron's expense. The baron in Source 6 points to himself to show that he will serve the king. The soldiers formed the king's army, to fight, or to protect castles.

> I will be your man from this day onwards for life and limb and loyalty. I shall be true and faithful to you for the lands that I hold from you.

SOURCE 7
The oath of homage made by the baron to the king.

In return, the barons gave some of their land to knights. Each knight swore an oath of homage to the baron and agreed to serve him as a fully-armed knight, with a horse, for 40 days a year. The knight was given land (a manor) to live on. The Church was also part of the feudal system as Source 8 shows.

Problems with the feudal system

There were three main problems with the feudal system.

- **The problem of the barons.** Sometimes barons became too powerful. They had their own castles and their own armies, and were like little kings (see Source 9). They could challenge the king himself (see Source 10).

- **The problem of the Church.** The Church was very powerful and looked to the pope, in Rome, for leadership. Many monarchs resented this.

- **The problem of the bad king.** When so much depended on the personality of the monarch, life was very difficult if he or she was a bad ruler.

We will look at examples of each of these three problems in turn.

> 'King William sends greetings to Aethelwig, abbot of Evesham from Winchester. I order you to call together your chief vassals. Tell them to bring the fully-armed knights they owe me and meet me in Clarendon at Whitsun. You yourself must come to me at that time and bring the five knights you owe me in return for the abbey's lands.'

SOURCE 8
This source shows part of a letter sent from William to Abbot Aethelwig in 1072.

SOURCE 9
Norman knights.

SOURCE 10
Henry I's nightmare. Henry was always afraid that the barons might rise up in rebellion against him.

Henry II (1154–1189)

Henry II was one of the most important kings of the early Middle Ages. At the age of 21 he became king of enormous lands in Britain and France (see Source 11) and was one of the most powerful monarchs of his time.

Henry II's government

Nowadays the government of Britain is based in London. In the Middle Ages the government of the country was based on a person, the monarch, not a place. This meant that the government followed the king wherever he was. If you had a complaint to make to the king, you had to follow him around the country until he had time to listen to you. He might fit you in after a day's hunting, or before he set sail across the Channel (see Source 12).

Kings governed England as if it were their own private estate. For example, the king looked upon the treasury as his own personal money. It was kept in his bedroom in an iron-bound box. As you can see in Source 13 the king and his household travelled with lots of slow-moving baggage wagons.

SOURCE 12
Norman kings were particularly fond of hunting.

SOURCE 11
The areas of France ruled by Henry II.

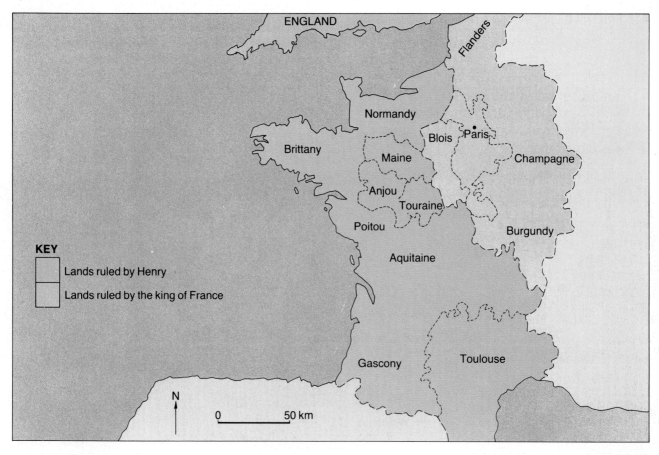

ENGLAND

Flanders

Normandy

Brittany

Blois · Paris

Maine

Champagne

Anjou

Touraine

Poitou

Burgundy

Aquitaine

KEY

☐ Lands ruled by Henry

☐ Lands ruled by the king of France

Gascony

Toulouse

N

0   50 km

SOURCE 13
Henry II and his household used to travel across the country regularly.

'Inquiry shall be made throughout each county through four law-abiding men of each town, on oath that they will tell the truth, if there is any man who is accused of being a robber or murderer or thief, or anyone who has sheltered robbers, murderers or thieves, since the lord king has been king.'

SOURCE 14
From the *Assize of Clarendon*, 1166.

The problem of the barons

England was in a terrible state when Henry II became king. There had been civil war since 1135 between Henry's mother Matilda and his uncle, Stephen. During the civil war the barons had become very powerful. It had become like Henry I's nightmare in Source 10. The barons had built castles without permission and kept their own soldiers. They used their soldiers to rob and murder innocent people.

Henry had to try to restore law and order. First he ordered all soldiers to return home by a certain date. Then he inspected all new castles, and ordered 300 of them to be pulled down.

The barons' law courts had also been used unfairly; the barons' friends escaped justice and innocent people were punished. Henry II therefore arranged for his own judges to travel around the whole country to hear disputes and punish criminals. A jury met to see which cases had to be heard before these travelling judges arrived (see Sources 14 and 15).

ACTIVITY

Work in groups of 12 for this improvised drama. The characters are: **a** three royal judges, who arrive in your area; **b** a jury of four; **c** wicked baron or baroness; **d** some villagers; **e** the barons' tough knights.

The scenes are:

1 The jury meets to discuss the forthcoming visit of the royal judges and the things the baron/baroness did during the civil war. Some villagers tell the jury the details of his/her bad deeds. The baron/baroness attends the meeting.

2 The jury meets the judges. It describes the crimes committed. The judges hear witnesses. They call on the baron/baroness to defend himself/herself. They reach a decision and pass sentence.

Note The judges have the king's support. If anyone abuses or disobeys the judges he/she is guilty of treason and can be executed and lose all his/her lands.

SOURCE 15
Judge and prisoners.

The problem of the Church

When Henry II tried to improve law and order in England he had to face the power of the Church courts. Anyone who was a member of the Church was not tried in a royal court, but in a Church court. Sometimes it was not just priests, but church bell-ringers, door-keepers, or anyone who could read who claimed this right. Often punishments delivered in Church courts were more lenient than Henry's judges would have given. Any appeals from Church courts went to the pope, in Rome, not to the king. The Church also offered SANCTUARY. This meant that criminals on the run could not be arrested if they took refuge in a church. The Church felt that people were often wrongly accused and that the barons' courts were cruel and unfair.

This conflict led Henry into one of the most famous quarrels between king and Church in the Middle Ages.

---

1 Why do you think this system of separate Church courts annoyed Henry II?

2 How do you think the Church would defend privileges like different courts, and sanctuary?

Thomas Becket

When Henry became king he found a clever man to help him rule. This man was Thomas Becket, the son of a London merchant, and in 1155 Henry made him chancellor. Becket was 15 years older than Henry, but they became firm friends, who went hunting and drinking together.

Becket had joined the Church in order to be educated, but he was not a very religious man. In 1161 the Archbishop of Canterbury, who was the head of the Church in England, died. Henry thought it would be a good idea to make his friend, Thomas Becket, Archbishop of Canterbury. Becket refused at first, because he thought it would lead to conflict, but Henry insisted. Becket became Archbishop in 1162 and immediately he changed (see Source 16).

'After Thomas became Archbishop, he turned from the power of the world and followed Christ. He wore a hairshirt of the roughest kind next to his skin; it reached to his knees and was covered in lice. He ate as little as possible and drank stale water.'

SOURCE 16
This source is taken from the *Chronicle of Herbert of Bosham*, for 1184.

Becket began to defend the rights of the Church and go against the wishes of the king. They quarrelled for several years until Christmas 1170, when Henry II finally lost his temper. Henry denied it later, but is supposed to have shouted in a temper: 'Will no one rid me of this turbulent priest!' We will never know whether he said this or not, but four knights set off from the King's court to carry out his command. They found Becket and murdered him at the altar of Canterbury Cathedral (see Source 17). His tomb soon became a place for pilgrims to visit and miracles are said to have happened there. In 1173 he was made a saint. You can read about Henry's reactions to the murder in Unit 4.

SOURCE 17
Murder of Thomas Becket in Canterbury Cathedral in 1170.

The problem of the bad king

King John is often regarded as the worst king England has ever had, as Sources 18 and 20 show.

Historians such as Stubbs based their opinions on chronicles written at the time. Most of the material we have is very critical of John (see Sources 19 and 21).

'The Church's corn was locked up and sold for the king. The king's men dragged priests of all kinds from their horses and robbed and beat them.'

SOURCE 21

This is from the *Chronicle of Roger of Wendover* for 1213.

'What marks out John from the long list of our kings and queens, good and bad, is that there is nothing in him that for a moment calls out for our better sentiments, nothing we can admire, nothing we can pity.'

SOURCE 18

This source was written by the historian Stubbs in 1873.

'King John imprisoned some of the barons' families and sent them to England in chains. He ordered them to be carefully guarded in Windsor Castle. One noblewoman, Matilda de Braose, died of starvation.'

SOURCE 19

This is from the *Chronicle of Roger of Wendover* for 1213.

attainment target 2

Read *all* the sources on this page and the sections on John and the Church and John and the barons on page 22 before you answer these questions.

1 What different impressions of John are given in Sources 18 to 21?

2 Suggest reasons for any differences in Sources 18 to 21.

3 Give one fact and one opinion from Sources 18, 19 and 21.

4 Why might the monk who wrote Sources 19 and 21 be hostile to John?

5 Does this mean that the impression given in Sources 19 and 21 might be inaccurate?

6 Sources 19 and 21 might be biased. Does that mean that Source 18 is also biased?

7 What is your opinion of John's relationship with the barons and the Church? What is your judgement of him?

8 Do you think John was **a** unlucky or **b** stupid or **c** wicked? Explain your choice. Compare your interpretation with Sources 18 and 20.

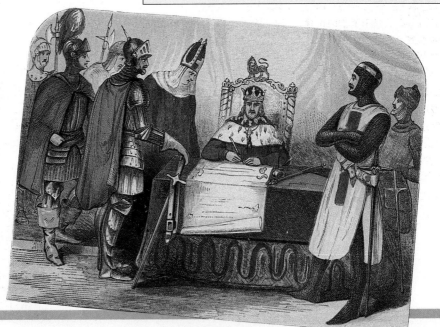

SOURCE 20

Illustration from a Victorian textbook, showing King John agreeing to Magna Carta.

John and the Church

John felt that he should have been allowed to choose his own archbishop as previous kings of England had done. The pope said that John had no right to do this. The quarrel lasted for years.

From 1208 to 1213 the pope put England under an INTERDICT. This meant that churches were locked, and there were no services.

John and the barons

In 1204 John lost most of the English lands in France to the French. He believed he had been unlucky in war, and that his allies had let him down. He claimed he needed to collect more taxes because the cost of war had risen. A soldier now cost 24d per day. Thirty years earlier the cost was only 8d per day. The barons, however, believed that John was not a good leader in times of war. They called him SOFTSWORD. They thought he taxed them too heavily and interfered in their affairs.

Modern historians, however, can prove that John was a hard-working king, who often travelled around his kingdom. He paid close attention to law and order and took care to collect all the money that was due to him.

Magna Carta

In 1214, the barons rebelled against John. By 1215 they had him in their power. Stephen Langton, who was the pope's choice as Archbishop of Canterbury, tried to persuade John to agree to terms which would bring peace. These terms were listed in a charter, which became known later as MAGNA CARTA, the great charter (see Sources 22 and 23).

1. If you look at Source 22 you can see that the charter covered many different topics. Make a list of those who benefited from each clause.

2. Did VILLEINS, serfs or women benefit from any of these terms?

3. Who is supposed to ensure that the king keeps his word?

1. The English Church shall be free and keep all its rights, including free election to senior posts.

2. If an earl or baron who holds land from the Crown dies, his heir shall take over the land at the standard payment to the king of £100 for an earl, £5 for a knight. (John had been claiming up to £1000.)

13. The City of London shall have all its ancient freedoms and customs by land and water as will all other cities, boroughs, towns and ports.

33. All fish weirs shall be removed from the River Thames and River Medway.

39. No free man shall be arrested, imprisoned, fined, outlawed, or attacked except after trial by his equals according to the laws of the land.

63. The barons shall choose a council of 24 people to see that the king keeps this charter.

SOURCE 22
Some of the 63 clauses of the *Magna Carta*.

SOURCE 23
Magna Carta.

However, John broke his word very quickly and the barons did not take Magna Carta seriously. War broke out again and was still going on when John died, suddenly, in 1216. His son and heir, Henry III, was only nine years old. Henry III's supporters made good use of the promises in Magna Carta. They re-issued it in 1216, and again in the following years. They saw it as a way of showing what a good, fair king Henry III would be.

As the centuries went by, people gave more importance to Magna Carta. They looked particularly at clause 39. This term seemed to be a guarantee to stop kings and dictators from throwing people into prison without trial. This may not have been what King John, Stephen Langton and the barons intended in 1215, but to this day the Magna Carta is still seen as an important foundation for people's freedom.

The origins of Parliament

The barons who rebelled in 1215 did not try just to defeat the king. They wanted to find a better way to govern the country and stop the king doing what he liked. A similar move happened later during Henry III's reign.

Henry III grew up to be a great patron of the arts. Many churches and cathedrals were built or improved in his reign, but he was less skilled as a ruler. The English barons particularly disliked him because he gave senior posts to his French friends. In 1258 the barons forced Henry III to call a Great Council. Some people also called it a parliament, from the French *parler*, to speak. The barons' leader, Simon de Montfort, wanted the king to pay attention and take note of the views of all kinds of English people. This Great Council included knights, as well as the barons and bishops. At first Henry accepted this, but in 1264 civil war broke out again. Simon de Montfort won a great victory at the battle of Lewes in 1265, and called a parliament. It was made up of barons, bishops and abbots, as usual, but also included two knights from every shire and two burgesses from every borough. The knights and burgesses later became the House of Commons.

Two hundred years after the Norman conquest, the government of England was starting to change. It now involved a much wider circle of people than the king and his barons, as you can see in Source 24.

In Source 24 find: the king, the two archbishops, other bishops, the peers (barons, earls) and members of the Commons.

In the Middle Ages Parliament was not very powerful. The king called Parliament, decided what it could discuss and sent it home. Sometimes years could go by before he recalled it. However, as you will see next year, it went on to become the most important part of British government.

SOURCE 24
Fifteenth century painting of Parliament in the Middle Ages.

Villages and towns

AIMS

In this unit we will find out more about the different groups of people who lived in England and Wales in the Middle Ages. In Unit 2 we learnt about kings, barons and famous people.

This unit looks at ordinary men, women and children, their lives and their work. Life in the villages was very different from town life. We will look at both and see how people lived. It is difficult to find out about unknown people who lived a long time ago. In this unit, we will examine some of the sources of evidence for this period and learn more about ordinary life in the Middle Ages.

It is very difficult to find out about the lives of ordinary people in Britain in the Middle Ages. We have few records of their daily lives, partly because most people could not write. The only record of individual names is usually for those people who were in trouble with the law.

Important people made sure their names were remembered by putting them on their tombs (see Sources 1 and 2). Sometimes we can see the kinds of things ordinary people did, if we study the sources, but we do not know who they were (see Sources 3 and 4).

In the Middle Ages most people in Britain lived in villages in the countryside. They went into town rarely. The knight in Source 1 had been on a crusade and had seen towns in many lands. When he was at home in England, however, he lived in his village. The people in Sources 3 and 4 would have spent most of their time in the village. Occasionally they went to a weekly market in a town, or to an annual fair. Only the merchant and his wife in Source 2 were familiar with the bustle of town life.

SOURCE 1
Tomb of Walter de Dunstanville, dated 1270. He was a knight and lord of the manor of Castle Combe, Wiltshire.

SOURCE 2
Brass from the tomb of William and Marian Grevel, 1401. William Grevel was a rich wool merchant from Chipping Campden, Gloucestershire.

gaudebunt campi z omnia que in eis sunt

SOURCE 3
Villagers cutting corn, 1340s.

1 Look at Sources 1 to 4. What can you learn about the different people from these sources?

2 Why do you think the people in Sources 1 and 2 had such expensive tombs made for them?

3 Why do you think we know the names of the people in Sources 1 and 2, but not of those in Sources 3 and 4?

SOURCE 4
Children watching a Punch and Judy Show, 1340s.

The English language

William I and his Norman followers spoke French, while the Anglo-Saxons continued to use a variety of Anglo-Saxon dialects in different parts of the country. For three hundred years after the conquest, French was the language of the rulers, but Anglo-Saxon was still the language of the ordinary people. The first king who spoke English as his first language was Edward III. He came to the throne in 1327.

This difference in social rank can still be heard in the English language today. For example, the people who looked after the animals were Anglo-Saxons, and used Anglo-Saxon words such as *cattle*, *swine* and *sheep*. The people who ate meat from these animals used the French words, *beef*, *pork* and *mutton*.

The Domesday Book

It took William I many years to conquer the whole of England. In Unit 2 you saw how he rewarded his followers with land in all parts of the country. However, he kept large areas of land for his own use. In 1085, he met with his Great Council in Gloucester and decided to find out about his new kingdom (see Source 5). Although it was very difficult to carry out the survey, the work was done. It was a record that was supposed to last for ever (that is until the day of DOOM). It was therefore known as the *Domesday Book*, which you can see in Source 6. No other country has a survey like it from the 11th century. No other such survey was carried out until 1801.

ACTIVITY

1 All the English words in the table below are borrowed from the French language. Copy out this table and write the words below in the correct column:

GOVERNMENT	THE ARMY	THE ARTS

parliament, prince, battle, music, poem, justice, paint, armour, duke, prison, costume, crown, colour, castle, punish, council, tower, beauty, court.

2 Explain why so many words in the English language to do with government, the army and the arts have a French origin.

---

1 Look at Source 5. Write down three things that the king wanted to find out about England.

2 Why would it be very difficult to carry out a detailed survey of every village, like the one in Source 5, in the 11th century?

3 The author of Source 5 does not seem to approve of this survey. Why?

'The king sent his men all over England into every county. He had them find out the size of the county, what land he owned himself, the cattle on the land and the taxes he ought to have every year from the serfs.

Also it was written how much each man had who was a landholder in England, in land or in cattle, and how much it was worth. So very accurately he caused it to be searched out, that there was not a single yard of land nor even, it is shame to tell, though it feared no shame to him to do, an ox, nor a cow, nor a swine was left that was not set down in his writing.'

SOURCE 5
An extract from the *Anglo-Saxon Chronicle* for 1085.

SOURCE 6
The *Domesday Book*.

Villages in the *Domesday Book*

Source 7 shows a page from the *Domesday Book*. It is written in Latin, with lots of abbreviations. In Source 7 you can see the information for three villages in Suffolk. Source 8 is a translation of the first village in Source 7. Source 9 gives us detailed notes on another place from a different part of the country. There is also a key to help you understand some of the words used.

It would seem that in 1086 Britain was a very different country from what it is today. It was a rural landscape of arable land, meadow and pasture, cattle and sheep and pigs. If you look at Source 9 you can see that the present city of Birmingham was worth less than the little Suffolk village of Risby shown in Sources 7 and 8. There were towns, but they were very small. The total value of the land of England was only £37,000.

If you look at Sources 8 and 9, you can see that the *Domesday Book* does not mention women, children or the clergy. In fact it mentions only male heads of households, about 280,000 people. The true population figure was probably five times the number of people who are mentioned in the *Domesday Book*.

'Suffolk. Sheet 14. Lands of the Abbey of St Edmund. THINGOE HUNDRED. Risby. St Edmund's held Risby as a manor before 1066. Two CARUCATES of land. Four VILLEINS. Two BORDARS. Then two ploughlands in the DEMESNE, now four. Always one plough land for the village men. Then three SERFS, now one. Meadow one acre. Three packhorses, 12 cattle, 30 pigs, 90 sheep, 32 goats. Seven FREEMEN with one carucate of land. The value of this manor at the time of King Edward was £4, now £6.'

SOURCE 8
This source is a translation of the entry for one of the villages in Source 7.

'Richard holds Birmingham of William Fitz Ansculf. Six carucates of land, one carucate in the demesne. Five villeins, four bordars. A wood half a mile long and four furlongs wide. In the time of King Edward it was worth 20s and it is still worth the same amount.'

SOURCE 9
This is the entry for Birmingham in the *Domesday Book*.

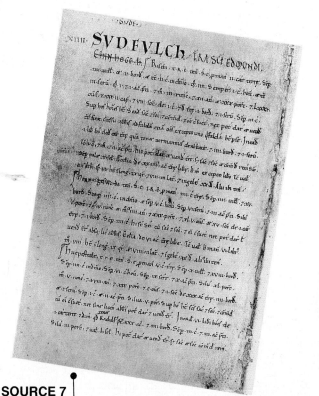

SOURCE 7
A page from the *Domesday Book* covering villages in Suffolk.

Key: Hundred = part of a county (about 20 to 30 villages)
Carucate = a measure of land (about 100 to 150 acres)
Villein = a villager with a reasonable amount of land, perhaps up to 30 acres
Bordar = a villager with a smallholding
Serf = a villager with no land, almost a slave
Demesne = the lord's land
Freeman = a villager who owned land

1 These *Domesday Book* entries in Sources 8 and 9 are the answers to the questions asked by William's officials in each village. Work out the questions which gave these answers.

2 What do Sources 8 and 9 tell us about William and his government officials?

3 Do you think the information in the *Domesday Book* is accurate? Give reasons for your answer.

4 Which kinds of people are *not* mentioned in Sources 8 and 9?

Village life

The *Domesday Book* gives us a picture of Britain as a land of villages. If you look at Source 10 you can see what one of these villages might have looked like.

Drawing of a village in the Middle Ages.

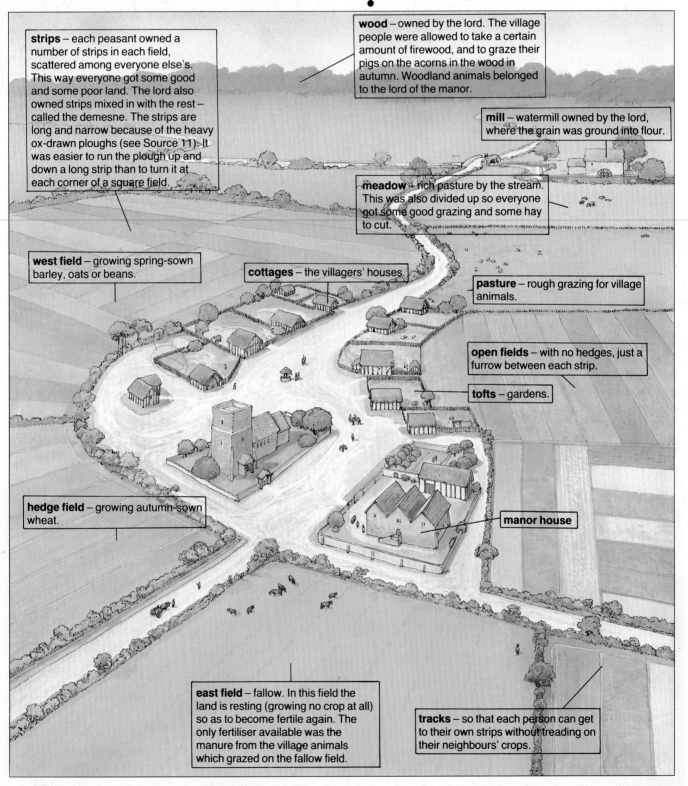

strips – each peasant owned a number of strips in each field, scattered among everyone else's. This way everyone got some good and some poor land. The lord also owned strips mixed in with the rest – called the demesne. The strips are long and narrow because of the heavy ox-drawn ploughs (see Source 11). It was easier to run the plough up and down a long strip than to turn it at each corner of a square field.

wood – owned by the lord. The village people were allowed to take a certain amount of firewood, and to graze their pigs on the acorns in the wood in autumn. Woodland animals belonged to the lord of the manor.

mill – watermill owned by the lord, where the grain was ground into flour.

meadow – rich pasture by the stream. This was also divided up so everyone got some good grazing and some hay to cut.

west field – growing spring-sown barley, oats or beans.

cottages – the villagers' houses.

pasture – rough grazing for village animals.

open fields – with no hedges, just a furrow between each strip.

tofts – gardens.

hedge field – growing autumn-sown wheat.

manor house

east field – fallow. In this field the land is resting (growing no crop at all) so as to become fertile again. The only fertiliser available was the manure from the village animals which grazed on the fallow field.

tracks – so that each person can get to their own strips without treading on their neighbours' crops.

Ploughing the land

As Source 10 shows, the land was divided up between the peasants who each farmed a number of strips of land in each field. In many parts of the country land had been divided and worked this way since the 5th and 6th centuries. The Normans hardly changed things at all. This system meant that people in the village had to work together. They had to plough the same field at the same time, harvest together and keep the animals under control. This was all organised by the REEVE, who was the village foreman.

SOURCE 12
Aerial photograph showing remains of medieval fields in Warwickshire.

Aerial photographs, taken in the late evening, can sometimes show up the strips of land, even though today they are in hedged fields. You can see evidence of such strips, if you look carefully at Source 12. You can see that the strips are slightly s-shaped, as the medieval ploughman began to turn his plough at the end of each furrow.

SOURCE 11
Ploughing in a medieval village.

1 Look at Source 10. In which ways were the peasants forced to work the land together?

2 In Source 10 what crops will be grown in each field next year?

3 Do you think the method of farming in Source 10 was fair for all those who worked the land?

4 Suggest ways in which the peasants could have worked the land more efficiently (for example, land not used well, time wasted, crop yields low etc).

5 Source 10 is a secondary source of evidence about a village in the Middle Ages. How would you check the accuracy of Source 10?

6 Why is it best to take a photograph, such as Source 12, in the late evening?

Working the land

In Unit 2 you saw how William I set up the feudal system by giving land to his Norman followers. In return, they had to fight for him. A similar agreement was made in the villages. Source 13 shows one such agreement. In practice it meant that most people in the village spent much of their time at work on the lord's demesne.

Life was very hard for villagers. They had to work long hours in the fields to grow enough food to live on. Serfs had no rights at all, whilst villeins and bordars were not their own masters.

1 In Source 13, which person has the best of the bargain?

2 In Source 14, how could the villein avoid some of his duties? Do you think he would have preferred to do this?

3 In Source 14, how did the lord benefit when he had the villein's sheep on his land?

4 Make a list of the things the lord could expect to receive from the villeins in Burton-on-Trent.

5 Source 13 is taken from a poem. Source 14 is an official document. What different kinds of evidence does each source provide?

'For my part, said Piers, I'll sweat and toil for us both as long as I live, and gladly do any job you want. But you must promise, in return, to protect me from thieves and robbers. You'll have to hunt down all the hares, foxes, boars and badgers that break down my hedges. You must tame falcons to kill the wild birds that eat my wheat.'

SOURCE 13
From the *Vision of Piers Plowman*, written by William Langland in the 1370s.

'There are eight villeins at Burton-on-Trent. Each villein works for two days each week for the lord. He provides the lord with a horse for one journey a year or pays a fine of four pence.
He must bring one cartload of wood. At Christmas he provides two hens and makes one barrel of malt. He ploughs twice a year. In summer he must put his sheep on the lord's enclosures. In August he must provide an extra man for reaping.'

SOURCE 14
This source shows a survey of the duties of villeins.

- The land did not belong to villeins and bordars, but to the lord.
- They had to work for the lord (see Source 13). This work was called LABOUR SERVICES.
- They had many other duties to the lord (see Source 14).
- They could not leave the village without permission.
- They could not buy or sell goods.
- They had to pay a fine to the lord if their daughters married.
- When a villein or bordar died a fine had to be paid to the lord before his heir could take over the villein's land.

SOURCE 15
A list of the rights of serfs, villeins and bordars showing the restrictions placed on them by the lord.

Village homes

In the Middle Ages the houses that villagers lived in were so small and badly built that very few have survived. In Source 16 you can see a villager's cottage.

Village houses did not have windows because glass was expensive. The floor was made of beaten earth, with an open fire on a stone slab in the middle. There was no chimney, so the cottage was often filled with smoke. Peasants had very little furniture just a few stools, a table, a few pots and a mattress to sleep on. Pigs, chickens, even goats and cows often lived in the cottage too.

Each cottage had a garden or TOFT (see Source 10) in which the villager could grow a few vegetables. A few chickens or other animals could be kept on the common. There was not enough

SOURCE 16
A villager's cottage from the Middle Ages.

food to feed all the animals during the winter, so most of them were slaughtered at Michaelmas (29 September). There were no freezers, so meat had to be eaten fresh, or else smoked or salted to preserve it. This meant that there was enough food to eat in late summer, but by the end of winter supplies were very low. For most of the year villagers ate very little meat. Bad weather often led to a poor harvest and deaths from starvation. The most common months for deaths were April and May.

Regional variations

Although most villages followed the pattern described in Source 10 there were variations in many parts of the country, as shown in Source 17. The pattern of farming you saw in Source 10 was common to the areas shown in blue. The areas shown in green were subject to the Forest Laws. This does not mean that they were all thickly forested, although some were. The main purpose of the Forest Laws was to protect land for the sport that William and his successors loved: hunting. When William died, a writer of the period wrote: 'He loved the deer, as if he were their father'. There were villages in some of these forests, but very little farming took place. The villagers made their living by providing timber for building, tools and fuel, and looking after the deer.

Areas marked in brown in Source 17 looked more like Source 18. Here, individual farmers had made their own fields out of the woodland. There were few villages, just scattered

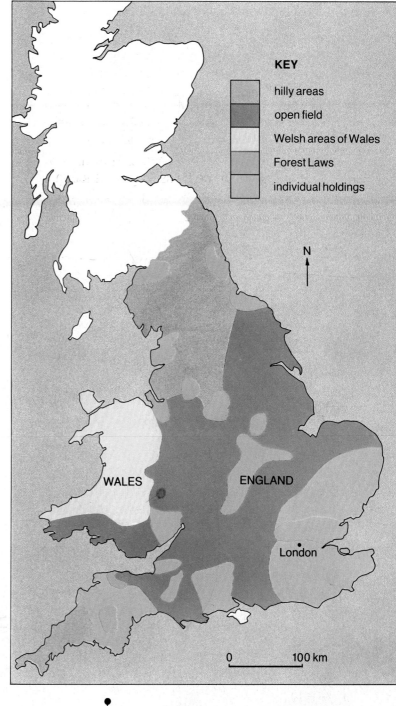

KEY

	hilly areas
	open field
	Welsh areas of Wales
	Forest Laws
	individual holdings

N

WALES   ENGLAND

London

0   100 km

SOURCE 17
Map showing different types of farming and land use.

farmsteads. In the more hilly areas marked in grey in Source 17 there was not enough room for large open fields. One or two small, open fields near the village were cultivated nearly every year, using lots of manure as fertiliser. The open hills beyond provided hundreds of acres of pasture, on which the small villages relied.

The lord of the manor

The lives of the lord, lady and their family were very different from the lives of the villeins and serfs. The number of servants ensured that the lord and his family rarely had to do any work as Sources 20 and 21 show. They lived in a manor house, or even a castle. This was much better built than the houses of the villagers, although still draughty and dirty by our standards. They had more, and better food.

SOURCE 18
Fields and scattered farms in Devon.

The Welshry of Wales, the area the Normans did not conquer, is marked in yellow in Source 17. The Welsh lived in small groups of farms called TREFI. Fifty trefi made up a cwmwd, which was like a large estate that combined highlands and lowlands, meadows and woods. There were quite a few serfs in Wales, but many Welsh people were free and belonged more to their family than to their lord. You can see a Welsh farm in Source 19.

'In the morning, before your lord shall rise, take care that his linen is clean. If the weather is cold, warm it at a clear fire, which is not smoky. When he rises, place a chair with a cushion on it before the fire and another cushion for his feet. Then ask your lord to come and be dressed.

First hold his tunic out to him, then his doublet while he puts in his arms. Then draw on his socks and hose and buckle his shoes. Put a kerchief around his neck and on his shoulders and then gently comb his hair with an ivory comb and give him water to wash his hands and face. Then kneel down and say thus: Sir, what robe or gown does it please you to wear today?'

SOURCE 20
An extract from an instruction book for servants from the 15th century.

1   How far do Sources 20 and 21 agree with each other?

2   Why do historians try to find more than one source on a subject?

SOURCE 19
Welsh farm.

SOURCE 21
A lord dressing in front of a fire.

SOURCE 22
Villagers could be fined for trying to trap rabbits in the lord's woods.

ACTIVITY

The Manor Court

Many lords hunted for much of their time, but they also had to govern their village. They did this by holding a court, usually in their manor house. The 'reeve' would report any villager who had broken the rules and customs of the village to the lord or lady. The villager would then be asked to defend himself or herself.

Work in groups of six. Your characters are:
a the lord or lady of the manor
b the reeve
c villagers 1, 2, 3 and 4.

Look at the rules and customs of a village on pages 28 to 31. Here are some more customs found in your village.

- Every villager should take a turn to look after the pigs when they are turned into the lord's woods to root for acorns. The penalty is a fine of 12 pence.

- Villagers are not allowed to play football. The penalty is a fine of half a mark (6s 8d, 33p). (Football was a very rough game at that time, with almost no rules; people were often injured.)

- All villagers should look after the road outside their houses.

Set up a court. The reeve explains to the lord or lady what the villager has done wrong. The villager can reply. The lord or lady makes a decision, and if he/she thinks the villager is guilty he/she decides on the punishment.

Here are some ideas to help you. The reeve accuses villagers 1 and 2 of the following crimes:
Villager 1 is a villein who took a day off work to visit members of his family in a nearby town.
Villager 2 is a serf, who was caught trapping rabbits in the woods (see Source 22). Add your own ideas for the accusations the reeve makes against villagers 3 and 4.

Women in the Middle Ages

Women had very little power in the Middle Ages. The Norman Conquest made their position worse. Those women who were members of the Anglo-Saxon ruling class were treated very badly. They had already lost fathers, sons, brothers, and husbands in the battles of 1066. Then William took their land to give to his Norman followers. Many women had to take refuge in nunneries (see Unit 4).

'Mother, I heard while I was in London there was a goodly young woman to marry, who was daughter to Seff, a merchant. She shall have £200 in money on her marriage and 20 marks per annum from land after the death of her stepmother who is 50 years of age. I spoke with some of the maid's friends and have got their good wills to have her married to my brother Edmund.'

SOURCE 23

Extract from a letter written by one of the Paston family, landowners in Norfolk, to his mother about a wife for his unmarried younger brother.

SOURCE 24

A 14th century picture of well-dressed upper-class women.

SOURCE 25

Chess was a popular game for upper-class women.

After the Norman Conquest, Norman law became the law of the land. This was much tougher on women than Anglo-Saxon law. For example, it became hard for women to own property. If a woman married, all her possessions belonged automatically to her husband. For this reason the marriages of wealthy people were often arranged by their parents. Women from these families were rarely consulted as to who they wished to marry, as you can see from Source 23.

Daughters of poor families seem to have been in a better position. There was no money involved so they were able to make their own choice of marriage partner. In some parts of Wales women were allowed to keep their own property. The old Welsh laws of HYWEL DDA allowed women to keep half of the property of a married couple if there was a divorce. (This did not happen in England until 1887.) Welsh customs also gave women the task of memorising their family history. This was important in Wales where people passed their property on, even to fifth cousins in some cases.

After they married, upper-class women could live an idle life, if they wished. They were not allowed to take part in government, war, or lawmaking. An upper-class woman could devote her time to thinking about clothes and playing games (see Sources 24 and 25).

Women with power

Many women in the upper classes did not, however, lead an idle life. They often had to run a large household and landed estate. Sometimes their husbands were away on business for weeks or, if they went on a crusade, for years. For example, Lady Alice de Brienne was Lady of the Manor of Acton, in Suffolk. As you can see in Source 26, she supervised her steward who kept her accounts and ran a large household.

Some evidence from the Middle Ages suggests that it was the women who were educated and who taught the children (see Source 27). In all social classes, women were given the important task of looking after children. Women helped each other at childbirth and cared for sick and elderly people. Without trained doctors most villagers relied on their 'wise women's' medical skills (see Sources 28 and 29).

'**Meals:** breakfast for 30, dinner for 160, supper for 30. **Guests:** William Sampson with his wife and one of his household, the wife of Robert Dynham with her son, Margaret Brydebeck, Agnes White, Agnes Lockwood with two sons, a daugher and a maid servant. **Pantry:** 314 white and 40 black loaves, wine and ales. **Kitchen:** Two pigs, two swans, 12 geese, two sheep, 24 chickens and 17 rabbits.'

SOURCE 26
Extract from the accounts of Lady Alice de Brienne, for New Year's Day, 1413.

SOURCE 27
Women often taught children to read.

SOURCE 28
Women looking after a young baby. At the front of the picture a female servant prepares the baby's food.

SOURCE 29
Women treating a sick man. This is taken from a 14th century illustration.

Peasant women

Peasant women had to work very hard. As you saw in Sources 3 and 11, women were expected to work in the fields. They also had to look after the home, children and prepare the food. Many women did other important jobs for the family, such as spinning, milking or keeping a few chickens (see Sources 30 and 31).

Peasant women had a vital role to play. Their skill at juggling the supply of money and food kept the whole family together. Marriages had to be partnerships. You can see in Source 32 how difficult life could be for peasant women in the Middle Ages. Source 33 shows, however, that some women still retained a sense of humour.

'A woman is a worthy thing,
They do the wash and do the wring,
Lullay, lullay, she doth sing
And yet she hath but care and woe.

A woman is worthy wight,
She serveth man both day and night,
Thereto she putteth all her might
And yet she hath but care and woe.'

SOURCE 32
This source is from a medieval song.

In 1267 William of Stansgate, who was carrying bows and arrows, met the widow Desiderata, a particular friend and the godmother of his son, in the street. She asked him in jest if he was one of the men appointed by the king to keep the peace. She declared she could overcome two or three men like him, crooked her leg, grabbed him up by the neck and threw him to the ground.

SOURCE 33
This extract from a medieval court record gives a rather different picture.

SOURCE 30
Woman feeding her hens and chicks. She has a distaff, used for spinning, under her arm.

SOURCE 31
Milking the cows was usually done by women.

Modern historians learn about village life by studying the evidence available. A French historian, E Le Roy Ladurie, studied the records of the village of Montaillou in Southern France, between 1295 and 1325. Source 34, which is based on his study of the records, gives us information about everyday life in the village. We can also learn about village life from Source 36.

- The peasants lived mainly on bread, with a small amount of cheese. They made thick soup with bacon, bread, cabbage, leeks and turnips. Meat was rare, except for smoked or salt pork.
- In 43 out of the 50 married couples in the village, both husband and wife came from Montaillou. There was one divorce in the 30 years studied.
- There was little or no education. Only four of the 259 villagers could read and write.
- There was one murder in the 30 years studied.

SOURCE 34
Some points from the work of the French historian, E. Le Roy Ladurie about Montaillou.

'As I went by I saw a poor man hanging onto a plough. His coat was of coarse material. His hood was full of holes and his hair stuck out of it. As he trod the soil his toes stuck out of his worn shoes. His wife walked beside him with a long goad. She wore a sheet to protect her from the weather. She walked barefoot on the ice so that the blood flowed. At the end of the row there was a little bowl and in the bowl lay a baby covered in rags. Two two-year-old children were on the other side and they all cried the same cry, a miserable note. The poor man sighed deeply.'

SOURCE 36
Extract from the *Vision of Piers Plowman* written by William Langland, a 14th century writer.

SOURCE 35
Women spinning with a spinning wheel.

attainment target 3

1 What do Sources 30, 31 and 35 tell us about the role of women in farming and family life in the village?

2 In what ways do Sources 32 and 36 agree about the role of women in village life?

3 In what ways does Source 33 give us a different picture of the role and character of women in the Middle Ages?

4 The author of Source 34 is not a medieval peasant, but a French historian from the 20th century. How might this affect the reliability of Source 34?

5 The author of Source 36 was not a peasant, but an educated writer. How might this affect the reliability of Source 36?

6 What would you want to know about E Le Roy Ladurie (Source 34) and William Langland (Source 36), in order to decide the reliability of Sources 34 and 36?

7 Which of Sources 30 to 36 are primary sources of evidence and which are secondary sources of evidence about life in the Middle Ages?

8 Choose three sources you would use to give a full account of village life in the Middle Ages to someone who knows nothing about it. Explain your choice.

9 In Source 34 we read that there was one divorce and one murder during a period of 30 years in Montaillou, and that most people married their neighbours. Does that mean that the villagers were happy?

Towns

Almost everything village people needed to live on could be provided by the village. Bread, ale, timber for houses and furniture, leather for shoes and woollen cloth for clothes, were all home-made. The village was almost SELF-SUFFICIENT. However, villagers had to buy salt to preserve food, metal for ploughshares, knives and other tools. These items had to be bought from a merchant at a market. To make the money to buy these goods villagers sold their surplus food, particularly eggs, butter and cheese, at the market. Where there were markets, towns started to develop (see Source 37).

Why did towns grow?

In 1086 there were only 20 towns in England with a population of over 1,000. Over the next 400 years towns grew in size and new towns were started. There were several reasons for this. During this period England was a fairly peaceful land. The population was growing, and there was a greater demand for goods. More people began to settle in towns. They specialised in making goods which they could sell, such as shoes, gloves, knives, clothes, hats and medicines. Those villagers who could afford to began to buy these goods and no longer made them themselves. Lords were very keen to develop towns because they made money from tolls and rents. They imposed certain customs and rules for those villagers who wanted to trade in the towns (see Source 38).

Sometimes lords provided a market cross for villagers to display their goods for sale (see Source 39). Later they sometimes built a market hall (see Source 40). In the market hall the ground floor was open so that stalls could be set up, protected from the weather. The rooms above were used by merchants and traders to discuss business, and by the Town Council.

Towns often grew up next to castles. The castle provided protection for the townspeople and the soldiers needed the towns to supply food. Lords often encouraged this. At Pembroke the castle protected the town's market (see Source 42). If you look at Source 42 you can see that the main street is much wider mid-way. This is where the market used to be held. In other towns, such as Devizes and Framlingham, houses clustered round the edge of the castle bailey.

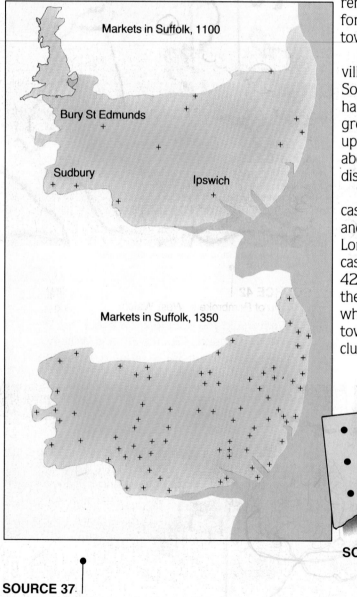

Markets in Suffolk, 1100

Bury St Edmunds

Sudbury

Ipswich

Markets in Suffolk, 1350

SOURCE 37
Map of market towns in Suffolk, 1100 to 1350.

- Every cart that comes into the city with fish for sale pays a rent of ½d.
- Every cart that brings iron or steel into the city pays a rent of 2d.
- Every tanner that owns a stall in the 'high market' pays ground rent of 2s.

SOURCE 38
This source gives us some of the customs of the city of Winchester.

SOURCE 39
Market cross at Ripley, in Yorkshire.

SOURCE 40
Market hall at Thaxted in Essex.

SOURCE 41
Open stalls of a tailor, a barber, a furrier and a grocer.

SOURCE 42
Town of Pembroke in West Wales.

Foreign trade

There was a demand for items that were not available in local towns. Norman lords were used to good wines, fine fabrics such as silk, and spices that they could not buy in England (see Source 43). The Norman Conquest brought England into greater contact with France. Soon English merchants were trading with many parts of Europe (see Source 44). This meant they had to trade by sea. If you look at Source 45 you can see two of the ships involved in sea-going trade. You can also see a packhorse, used to carry goods on land. In order to buy the goods shown in Source 43, English merchants had to have items to sell. In the early Middle Ages, England mainly exported wool. Then gradually cloth became the leading export item (see Source 46).

1 In Source 43, Alice de Brienne's steward called all the items listed 'spices'. Which items are not spices?

2 Look at Source 26. Why do you think she needed such large amounts of spices?

3 There is very little sugar in Source 43. How do you think Alice's cook sweetened food?

4 The ships in Source 45 were very small. How did this help them to reach towns that were some distance from the sea?

5 In Source 45, in what ways is a packhorse a better way to carry goods overland than a horse and cart?

6 Look at Source 46. Draw a graph to show the change in export patterns.

7 Use a calculator to work out how many sheep provided wool for export in 1350.

8 The king encouraged the change in exports from wool to cloth. Suggest reasons why he did this.

'Three pounds of pepper
Two pounds of ginger
Two pounds of cinnamon
Two pounds of cloves
Forty pounds of almonds
Four pounds of rice
Two bushels of mustard seeds
Six pounds of dates
Ten pounds of raisins
One pound of sugar.'

SOURCE 43
Extract taken from the household book of Alice de Brienne from 1413, showing the demand for spices not available in local towns.

SOURCE 44
Overseas trade of England in the 15th century.

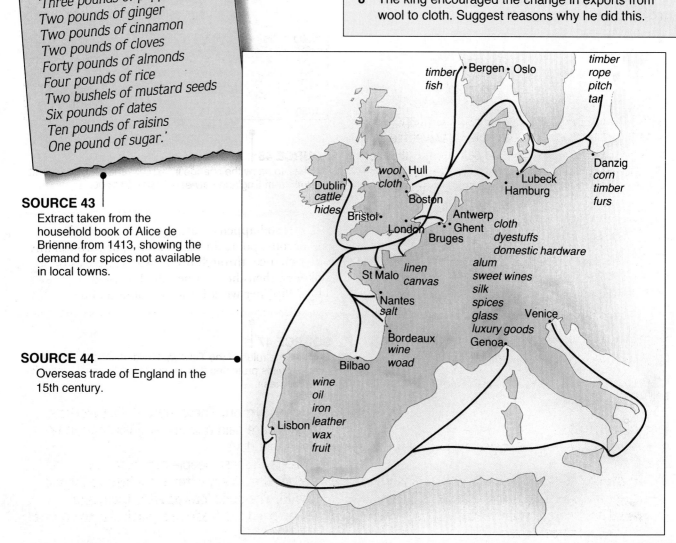

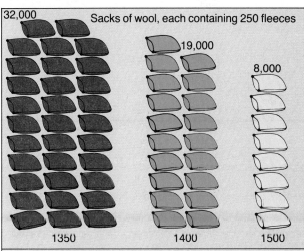

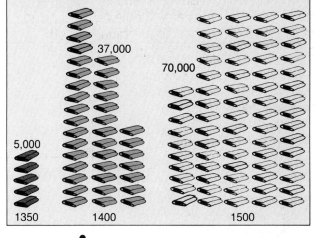

SOURCE 45
A port in 1400.

Townspeople

If you look back to page 30, you will see that villeins led very restricted lives in the villages. Town traders needed to be able to travel freely, to own goods and to buy and sell them. Villeins, therefore, were not allowed to trade. Unlike villeins townspeople were free. Towns were like little islands of freedom in a sea of lords and villeins. If a villein escaped to a town and lived there for a year and a day, he was given his freedom. These people were known as BURGESSES.

Townspeople had other rights too. They had the right to hold a market, or fair, to collect tolls and run their own law courts to try offenders. They might even have had their own town council. These rights were usually included in a CHARTER, a document which listed the freedoms given by the lord.

Town workers

There were usually three types of workers in towns.

1 **Apprentices.** These were young people who learnt a trade. They started at 12 years of age. They served seven years, and often lived in their master's house.

SOURCE 46
Chart to show the change in export patterns of wool and cloth from England between 1350 and 1500.

> If it so happens that any of the members become poor, through old age, or through any other chance, through fire or water, thieves or sickness, then the member shall be paid 11½d (5p) per week from the common box.

SOURCE 47
From the rules of the Tanners Guild of London, showing how guilds protected their members in times of hardship or sickness.

2 **Journeymen.** These were skilled workers, who were paid by the day (French *journée* means a day).

3 **Master.** These people ran their own businesses. They often combined to form a guild. The guild looked after them and controlled the trade in a particular town (see Source 47).

The power of the Church

In this unit we will find out about the religious beliefs of people in the Middle Ages. The fact that almost everyone believed in the teachings of the Church gave the Church great religious power. This unit also examines how the Church became powerful in other ways. We will see how the Church's control over money, land, the law and education led to criticisms of its actions by the end of the Middle Ages.

In Source 1 you can see York Minster which dominates the city as it has done since the 11th century. York Minster took 250 years to complete. Craftspeople were brought from all over Europe to work on the cathedral to make it beautiful. Source 1 shows that the Church had great power in the Middle Ages. The main reason for this was because people worried about life after death, as you can see in Source 2.

The speaker of Source 2 was an Anglo-Saxon lord discussing with King Edwin of Northumbria whether they should become Christians. The problem with life, as he saw it, is that it is very short and we don't know what came before our life or what will happen after we die. People took these problems very seriously in the Middle Ages. They believed that the answers the Church gave to their questions were correct. Their religious beliefs affected everyone, from peasants to kings, and every aspect of life.

Many people went on at least one PILGRIMAGE in their lives. This is a long journey to a place of religious importance. During the pilgrimage, pilgrims bought cheap badges like the one in Source 3, to show where they had been. For most people this was the only long journey that they would make in their whole lives.

SOURCE 1

The north side of York Minster, the 11th century cathedral in York.

1 What does Source 1 tell us about the wealth of the Church?

2 What does Source 1 tell us about the power of the Church?

3 What does Source 1 tell us about the beliefs of people in the Middle Ages?

Other people wanted to give their whole lives to God. They became monks or nuns. This meant they had to submit to strict rules. For example, they were not allowed to have any possessions of their own and had to keep their hair short. Source 4 shows a girl who is preparing to become a nun.

'When we compare our life on earth with the length of time before we live and after we die, about which we know nothing, it seems to me like the flight of a sparrow through a banqueting hall. You are sitting at dinner on a winter's day. In the middle is a comforting fire to warm the hall. Outside, the storms of winter rain or snow are raging. The sparrow flies quickly through one door of the hall and out of the other door. While it is inside it is safe from the wintry world from whence it came.

So we appear on earth for a little while, but of what went before this life, or of what follows, we know nothing.'

SOURCE 2
Extract from the *History of the English Church and People* by Bede, from the seventh century.

SOURCE 3
Pilgrim badge. Pilgrims bought these badges when they went on pilgrimages to show they had been.

SOURCE 4
Girl preparing to become a nun.

Religious beliefs

Look back to Source 2. Life after death worried people in the Middle Ages. Their lives were short and disease and death were commonplace. What would happen when they died? How should they live their lives? The answers to these questions were clear to the villagers of Chaldon in Surrey, whenever they went to church. Painted on the wall of their church was the DOOM or judgement you can see in Source 5.

If you look at Source 5, you can see that the angel, on the left-hand side of the picture, has a list of everything you have done throughout your life. If you have done good deeds you climb the ladder to Heaven. If you have done bad deeds, you go to Hell. In Hell, as you can see, devils tormented you.

This must have been very frightening for most people, but the Church claimed it alone could help you to earn a place in Heaven. Any wicked deeds you had committed could be forgiven if you confessed them to a priest.

He then made you do a PENANCE, a type of punishment which earned you forgiveness. Even kings had to do this. In 1174 Henry II came to Canterbury to do penance for the murder of Thomas Becket (see Source 6).

SOURCE 5
This doom or judgement is painted on the wall of Chaldon Church in Surrey.

SOURCE 6
This extract from a chronicle of 1174 shows Henry II doing penance for the murder of Thomas Becket.

'The king walked to St Thomas' tomb, barefoot. He was wearing only a woollen smock. He lay flat on the ground and then bishops, abbots, and the monks of Canterbury beat him. He stayed all that day and night and prayed in front of the martyr's tomb.'

---

1. What kinds of things happen to people who, according to Source 5, have done wicked things?

2. What is Hell like according to Source 5?

3. What does Source 6 tells us about the power of the Church?

4. Suggest reasons why Henry II did penance.

A piece of true cross, a bit of Christ's robe, some hairs from his beard, a piece of the pillar at which he was whipped, a thorn from his crown, a piece of the manger, St William's shoe, St Agatha's thigh bone, one of St Philip's teeth, and part of St Mary the Egyptian.

SOURCE 7
A list of relics to be found at Wimborne Minster in Dorset.

Relics

Most people believed in the power of religion to change their lives, and stories of miracles were common.

The Church had many special objects, often the remains of saints, which were believed to have supernatural powers. People believed these objects could pardon you, cure your illness, or give you something you wanted. These were called relics (see Source 7). Many people in the Middle Ages made pilgrimages to see important relics. Their beliefs added to the mystery and power of the Church.

The Parish Church

A priest looked after a village and its people. This was known as a PARISH. Priests were responsible to bishops who were grouped under an ARCHBISHOP. Archbishops in turn were responsible to the pope, in Rome, who was head of the ROMAN CATHOLIC Church. England, therefore, was just a small part of the international Church.

The parish church was the most important building in the village (see Source 8). It was certainly very different from the small, dark smokey huts in which most people lived. It was huge, peaceful, beautiful, and impressive. It did not have the rather plain walls and rows of pews you find in a church today.

The walls were painted with dramatic stories like the one in Source 5. There was usually a brightly-painted screen across the middle of the church, which separated the NAVE, where the people were, from the CHANCEL, where the priest conducted the service. You can see a screen in Source 9. There were seats for the rich, while a few stone benches at the side were reserved for the old and the ill. Most people stood or knelt in the open space (see Source 10). The priest took the service in Latin. This added to the sense of mystery, as very few people in the village

SOURCE 8
Parish church of Alfriston, East Sussex.

SOURCE 9
Screen of Cullompton Church in Devon.

SOURCE 10
Interior of Grosmont Church, showing where most people would have stood or knelt during a church service in the Middle Ages.

understood Latin. Everyone went to church on Sundays, as well as on saint's days. The local church was also the centre for most important events in life, such as weddings, baptisms, and funerals (see Sources 11 and 12).

SOURCE 11
Priest conducting a marriage service.

ACTIVITY

Use a whole page to copy out this diagram. Choose eight reasons why the Church was at the centre of village life. Write one word or draw a picture for each in the remaining eight boxes.

	🏠	

The church building was also the centre for many other activities. The priest sometimes taught village children to read and write so there might have been chairs and books. Fire-fighting ladders and hooks, weapons and armour and other spare equipment were also sometimes stored there. On occasion, tables were set up at the back of the church and feasts held to raise money. These events were known as 'church ales' and local people often went home rather drunk. There were no newspapers, radio or TV. The church was therefore a good way to find out what was going on in the village. Neighbours would exchange gossip and government proclamations or local notices would be read out.

The priest was a very important person. He was usually the only educated person in the village. He had his own land, called the GLEBE. He also received a TITHE (one-tenth) of all that the village produced. He did not marry, but usually had a good house of his own (see Source 13).

SOURCE 12
Priest baptising a baby.

SOURCE 13
A priest's house at Alfriston, East Sussex. This house dates from the 14th century.

Monasteries

For some people going to Church every Sunday was not enough. They wanted to devote their whole lives to God. DEVOUT Christians have a tradition of cutting themselves off from the rest of the world to concentrate on God. At first, people would live somewhere on their own in a remote area. In the 6th century, St Govan, for example, built a little cell on the Welsh coast (see Source 14). Later, whole communities of monks or nuns were set up. In the 6th century St Benedict laid down rules for these communities. One of these communities was Tintern Abbey in Source 15. This large abbey is beside the River Wye in South Wales.

Monasteries had very strict rules as Source 16 shows. When monks or nuns joined the monastery they had to take three vows: **poverty**, **chastity** and **obedience**.

SOURCE 14

St Govan's cell in Pembrokeshire on the Welsh coast.

SOURCE 16

Extract from the Rule of St Benedict emphasising **poverty**.

'No one shall call anything his own, no book, writing paper nor pen. Nothing at all. Let the brothers be given clothes that suit the weather. In normal places a cloak and hood will be enough. Monks must not grumble about the colour of rough cloth of their dress.'

SOURCE 15

A plan of Tintern Abbey in Wales.

The Abbey Church, built 1269–1301, replacing a much smaller one. Lay brothers and visitors sat in the nave (to the right); the monks sat in the choir (east end – to the left), where the altar was.

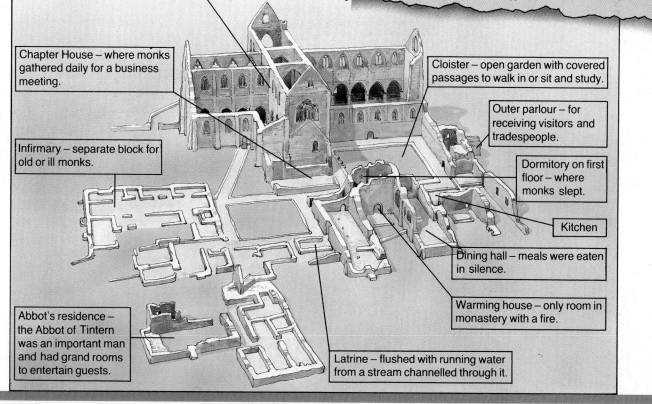

Chapter House – where monks gathered daily for a business meeting.

Cloister – open garden with covered passages to walk in or sit and study.

Outer parlour – for receiving visitors and tradespeople.

Infirmary – separate block for old or ill monks.

Dormitory on first floor – where monks slept.

Kitchen

Dining hall – meals were eaten in silence.

Warming house – only room in monastery with a fire.

Abbot's residence – the Abbot of Tintern was an important man and had grand rooms to entertain guests.

Latrine – flushed with running water from a stream channelled through it.

Monks and nuns stayed in the monastery or nunnery all the time. They did not marry or meet members of the opposite sex (**chastity**). The head of the community was the ABBOT, or ABBESS (in some places it was the PRIOR or PRIORESS). He or she had to be obeyed at all times. All the rules of the community had to be obeyed too (**obedience**). For example, most of the day was spent in silence. Meal times were silent except that one person would read out loud from the BIBLE (see Source 19). It was obviously difficult to communicate in silence. If anybody needed anything he would use sign language.

The main purpose of life in a monastery or a nunnery was prayer. As you can see in Source 15, the church was by far the largest and grandest building at Tintern Abbey. Here, services were held at 3 am, 6 am, 7 am, noon, 1.30 pm, 4 pm, and 6 pm. The dormitories in many monasteries had special 'night stairs', so that the monks could go straight from their beds into church for the services at 3 am and 6 am (see Source 18). Meals were taken at 7.30 am and 2 pm and there was a meeting in the CHAPTER HOUSE at 10 am. Monks slept from 7 pm to 3 am and from 4 am to 6 am. The rest of the time was devoted to work, reading or to private prayer.

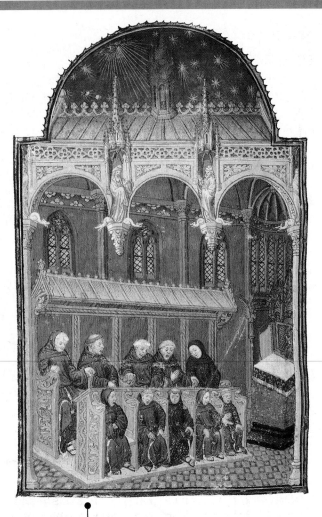

SOURCE 17
Monks in the monastery church.

SOURCE 18
Night stairs at Hexham Abbey. These stairs enabled the monks to go straight from their beds into church.

SOURCE 19
Nuns at a meal.

Work

There were lots of jobs to be done and monks and nuns were expected to work hard. Many monks and nuns grew their own food and had to tend the garden. As part of their service to the outside world they looked after travellers and people who were ill. Many of them were experts in making medicines.

One of the most important tasks was to write books. Printing was not known in Europe at this time, so every new book had to be written out by hand. It could take a scribe up to 18 months to write out a new *Bible* (see Source 20).

SOURCE 20

A monk writing with a quill pen. He has a knife for scraping away mistakes.

ACTIVITY

1   Use Sources 14 to 20 to design a daily timetable for a monk or nun. It could be set on a 24-hour clock. Services lasted about an hour except for the ones at 1.30 pm and 6 pm, which were usually half an hour in length.

2   If you had to be silent at meals, what signs would you use? Work out some signs in pairs, then try them on other people.

3   What do you think was the most difficult aspect of being a monk or nun?

SOURCE 21

Monks and nuns playing a game together.

Monastic orders

There were several different types of monasteries and nunneries known as ORDERS. Each order had slightly different rules.

1   **Benedictines:** This was the oldest order and followed the original rule of St Benedict. Benedictines wore black habits and were often attached to cathedrals.

2   **Cluniac:** This order was supported by William the Conqueror and the Normans.

3   **Cistercians:** They wore white habits and built their monasteries away from towns or villages, in order to lead a quiet simple life. Monks at Cistercian abbeys such as Fountains and Rievaulx in Yorkshire, Tintern Abbey in Source 15 and Strata Florida in Wales, began to tame the wild places where they settled. They became successful sheep farmers.

4   **Friars:** Orders of friars were started in the 13th century, with very strict rules about possessions. They worked among the poor in towns, and some were great preachers.

Church power on Earth

As we have already seen, the Church controlled people's religious beliefs throughout their lives and influenced their thoughts on what happened to them when they died. In the Middle Ages the Church also had tremendous power over other aspects of life as well.

Land

We saw in Unit 2 that William the Conqueror gave large amounts of land to the Church. Over the years the Church received more and more land until by the end of the Middle Ages, it owned about one-third of England and Wales. Source 22 shows pasture land belonging to Glastonbury Abbey, which the monks had created by draining the marshes. In practice for many people by the late Middle Ages the Church was their landlord or employer.

Money

The Church was very rich. The huge barn in Source 23 was built to store wheat from nearby farms. Some of the SHRINES on pilgrimage routes were very elaborate as Source 24 shows. Some Cistercian monasteries were also very rich from their connections with the international wool trade.

SOURCE 22
Glastonbury Abbey drained this land in Somerset, turning it into pasture.

'A wooden canopy covers the shrine. When that is drawn up with ropes, great treasures are open to view. The least valuable part is gold; every part glistened, shone and sparkled with rare and very large jewels. Some of these exceeded the size of a goose's egg.'

SOURCE 24
Description of the riches seen by one visitor to Thomas Becket's shrine at Canterbury.

SOURCE 23
Cressing wheat barn.

International organisation

The Church was an international organisation. It had a bishop in every diocese and a priest in every parish. The Church gradually became more powerful than even the monarchy (see Source 25). Successful men in the Church were able to work anywhere in Europe. Nicholas Breakspear was the only Englishman ever to become pope, in 1154. He had, however, previously been an abbot in France, papal ambassador in Scandinavia and a bishop in Italy.

Education

Almost all books were made by monks and most libraries were in monasteries or cathedrals. All schools and universities were run by the Church (see Source 26).

SOURCE 25
A painting to show the organisation of the Church.

SOURCE 26
A teacher with his pupils. He used to beat them with a birch.

attainment target 1

Look back over the whole of this unit to answer the following questions.

1 Give an example of the Church's importance in life based on what people believed.

2 Give an example of the Church's importance in life based on its power on earth.

3 Is there any link between your two examples?

4 The Church was important to different people in different ways. What do you think each of the following people would regard as the most important reason for the power of the Church:

a a villager with a strong religous belief?
b a villein with a bad back, who wanted to be cured?
c a serf on land that belonged to a nunnery?
d a stonemason who was building part of a new cathedral?
e an intelligent boy from a poor family?
f a king or queen?

5 What do *you* think was the most important reason for the power of the Church in the Middle Ages?

Criticisms of the Church

It was not surprising that many people criticised the Church. It was an organisation that was supposed to be simple and holy, but had become rich and powerful. There were many criticisms of bishops, monks and nuns as you can see in Sources 28 and 29.

> *Dames Isabel Benet and Agnes Halesley, nuns of Catesby, will not obey the orders of the bishop. Also the same Dame Isabel spent last Monday night with the Friars of Northampton. She danced and played the lute with them until midnight.*

SOURCE 27

Nuns and friars did not always obey the orders of the Church as this extract from Alnwick's *Visitations of Religious Houses* shows.

1 In what ways does Source 28 criticise bishops?

2 In what ways does Source 29 criticise the monk?

SOURCE 28

This 14th century carving shows a fox in bishop's clothing.

SOURCE 29

Illustration of the cellarer from a medieval manuscript.

In the 14th century Geoffrey Chaucer wrote a long poem in English. It told of a group of pilgrims travelling from London to Canterbury. Each pilgrim told a story to entertain the other members of the party. Chaucer's descriptions of the pilgrims themselves also gives us interesting evidence. Several pilgrims were members of the Church. They included a monk and a prioress in Sources 30 and 31. We can see from these sources that neither of these two pilgrims was very religious. Chaucer made jokes about his pilgrims' worldly habits and greed for possessions.

This shows that attitudes to the Church were changing. John Wycliffe, who was a teacher at Oxford University at this time, made a more serious attack on the Church. He criticised the power and wealth of the Church, and urged bishops, monks and nuns to give up their riches and lead simple lives. He also wanted ordinary people, who had not learnt Latin to be able to read the *Bible*. He arranged for the *Bible* to be translated into English. This translation came out in 1382. Wycliffe's followers, called LOLLARDS, were arrested, tried and burnt, but Wycliffe's ideas and his *Bible* remained. Next year you will see how they became an overwhelming force in the 16th century.

The monk

'This monk was therefore a good man to horse
Greyhounds he had, as swift as birds, to course.
Hunting a hare, or riding at a fence,
Was all his fun, he spared for no expense.

I saw his sleeves were garnished at the hand
With fine grey fur, the finest in the land.
He was not pale like a tormented soul,
He liked a fat swan best, and roasted whole.'

SOURCE 30
Extract from Chaucer's *Prologue to the Canterbury Tales*.

The prioress

'She had little dogs she would be feeding
With roasted flesh, or milk, or fine white bread.
And bitterly she wept if one were dead
Or someone took a stick and made it smart.
She was all sentiment and tender heart.
Her cloak, I noticed had a graceful charm.
She wore a coral trinket on her arm.'

SOURCE 31
Extract from Chaucer's *Prologue to the Canterbury Tales*.

SOURCE 32
This carved beam from the Cistercian abbey at Cleeve, Somerset, shows the wealth of the order.

SOURCE 33
Portrait of John Wycliffe.

1 In Source 30, what are the monk's clothes and interests in life?

2 What do you think a monk should be like?

3 In Source 31, what are the prioress' clothes and interests in life?

4 In Source 31, in what ways does the prioress fail to live up to the rules of her order?

Kings and nations

AIMS

In 1066 the four lands of England, Scotland, Ireland and Wales were separate countries. In this unit we will see how England gradually came to dominate the other countries. We will examine the feeling of belonging to a nation, or country and look at the development of nationhood over these years. We will find out about people whom the English, Scottish, Irish and Welsh still look upon as heroes. This unit also helps us to understand relations between the four countries that make up Great Britain.

The football fans in Source 1 all support the same football team. They think their team is the best; they want it to win every time. Where do your strongest feelings of belonging lie? Are they with your school, your football team or the place where you live?

Are you Cornish, East Anglian, a Northerner, a Londoner, a Brummie or a Scouse? Are you Irish, Scottish, Welsh, English or none of these?

At the time of the Norman Conquest people did not feel they belonged to a nation, or to a country. They felt they belonged to their family, to their village, and to their lord, to whom they had sworn an oath of homage. People felt only a vague sense of loyalty to their king, whom most of them rarely saw. Even kings thought of their lands as their estates, not their country. Throughout the early Middle Ages the kings of England were also rulers of huge lands in France as you can see in Source 2. They spoke French. Some kings visited England very rarely. Richard I, called the 'Lion-Heart', spent only six months in England in the ten years of his reign, 1189 to 1199, (see Source 3).

SOURCE 1

Terrace of English football fans, all supporting their team in the World Cup.

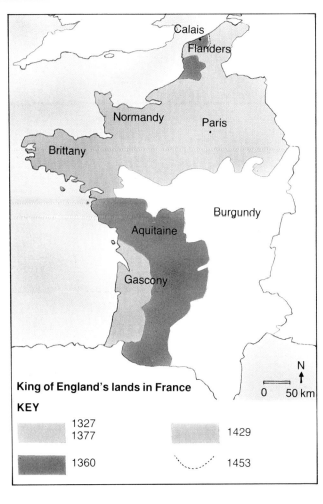

SOURCE 2
English lands in France during the later Middle Ages.

King of England's lands in France
KEY

1327 1377	1429
1360	1453

SOURCE 3
Richard the Lion-Heart's statue outside the Houses of Parliament in London.

'The English will never honour their king unless he is victorious and loves fighting. They war against their neighbours, especially those who are richer than themselves. They thoroughly enjoy battles and slaughter.'

SOURCE 4
Extract from the chronicles by the French writer Jean Froissart showing the barons' love of war.

SOURCE 5
Soldiers often attacked and looted the homes of villagers.

As we saw in Unit 2 most of the territories in France that belonged to England were lost in the reign of King John. Over the next 100 years, English kings paid more attention to Wales and Scotland. However, in the 14th century English kings turned again to try to recapture their French lands. The English were at war with France for over a 100 years between 1337 and 1453.

Another reason for these continuous wars was that barons expected to spend their lives at war (see Source 4). Such wars had a devastating effect on the lives of ordinary people. Source 5 shows soldiers about to attack and loot a villager's house, an event which was all too common in the French wars. In this unit, however, we will concentrate on the wars waged by kings and barons in Britain.

The Normans in Wales

As you can see from Source 6, Wales is a very hilly country with two thirds of the land over 200 metres above sea level. When William the Conqueror came to England in 1066, Wales was a separate country with its own laws and its own language. The Welsh often made raids across the border into England. They would come down to the rich farmlands on the English side of the border and seize grain, cattle and horses. William therefore gave special powers to three of his trusted Norman barons in these areas: William Fitz Osbern at Hereford, Roger of Montgomery at Shrewsbury, and Hugh of Avranches at Chester. He gave them large amounts of land on the English side of the border and told them that if they wanted to they could take land from the Welsh. Source 6 shows how much land the barons gained on the Welsh side of the border.

These barons were known as MARCHER LORDS, and they became little kings in their own areas. ('Mearc' is an old English word for a boundary.) Source 7 shows one of the castles they built. They also raised their own armies, ran their own law courts, and had their own jails. In some places, they set up monasteries with Benedictine monks. Where possible, they set up towns next to their castles.

In 1108 Henry I, the English King, increased his power in South west Wales when he sent settlers to live there. The settlers were protected by Pembroke Castle. They were mainly Flemings, from the Low Countries, with some English people from Somerset and Devon. Henry appointed Normans as bishops in Wales to help the English resettle the area.

In Pembrokeshire (now part of Dyfed) the boundary is still very obvious to this day (see Source 8). It is called the LANDSKER. People south of the boundary speak English and live in places called Johnston, Steynton, Uzmaston and Wiston. Villages have a parish church, a village green, a vicarage, an inn and perhaps an old castle. In the fields you can still see the remains of the old open-fields and strips. Those people who live north of the line are more Welsh speaking to this day. There are few villages, but scattered farms and hamlets such as Treffynon, Pont-yr-Hafod and Blaen-Llyn. The land is usually moorland, with small sheep-farms.

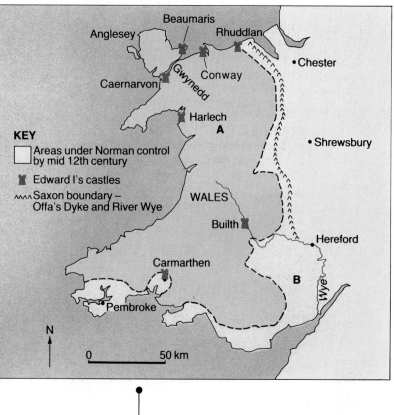

SOURCE 6

Map of Wales. Two-thirds of the land is over 200 metres above sea level.

KEY

- Areas under Norman control by mid 12th century
- Edward I's castles
- Saxon boundary – Offa's Dyke and River Wye

SOURCE 7

White Castle in Gwent. This castle was probably started by William Fitz Osbern and later strengthened by the Earls of Hereford.

South of the line is the area taken by English settlers in 1108, encouraged by Henry I. The countryside looks very English. To this day this area is known as 'little England beyond Wales'.

North of the line is the area left to the Welsh. It is rougher, higher land. To this day it is more Welsh-speaking.

For years after the English came the two peoples often fought each other. The boundary between them moved according to who was winning. Only after many years did it settle along the line shown on the map.

SOURCE 8
The landsker in Pembrokeshire. The boundary divides former English and Welsh areas.

The marcher lords and Ireland

Ireland at this time was a divided land. The last 'High King of all Ireland' was killed in battle in 1014. After his death local chiefs and kings continued to quarrel among themselves. The Church in Ireland suffered because of these quarrels and in 1155 the pope made Henry II overlord of Ireland. He hoped Henry would use this title to bring order. Henry, however, did nothing.

In 1156, Dermot, who was king of Leinster, a province of Ireland, appealed to an English marcher lord, Richard de Clare, Earl of Pembroke for help in his wars. Richard de Clare, who was also known as Strongbow, agreed. From 1169 to 1170 Strongbow and his soldiers helped Dermot to regain his kingdom. When Dermot died Strongbow became king of Leinster. Henry II obviously did not want one of his barons to be crowned king where he was supposed to be overlord. So in 1171 to 1172 Henry visited Ireland and made all the Irish kings, including Strongbow, accept his rule.

This was, however, shortlived. Over the next 50 years other marcher lords also carved out kingdoms for themselves by conquering parts of Ireland. There was little the English kings could do. King John visited Ireland twice and forced all its kings to submit to him, but again this did not last long. For the rest of the Middle Ages, Ireland remained part conquered and subject to English rule and part independent. Eventually the barons pleased themselves whether they were loyal to English kings. One area alone followed English law. This was known as the Pale, the area around Dublin.

SOURCE 9
Bunratty Castle, one of the Norman castles in Northern Ireland.

Edward I and Wales

In the 13th century the rulers of Gwynedd in north west Wales, began to emerge as supreme rulers over all of Wales. Gwynedd was a mountainous area of Wales. This meant it was safe from attack by the English. At the same time the fertile island of Anglesey provided it with a good supply of grain.

In 1272 Edward I became King of England. He was determined to rule the whole of Britain. However, Llywellyn, prince of Gwynedd, was equally determined to insist on his independence. He wrote to Edward and told the English king not to meddle in Welsh affairs. Llywellyn also refused to attend Edward's coronation and to give homage to Edward as his overlord.

Edward planned to teach Llywellyn a lesson. In the summer of 1277, after careful preparation, Edward attacked. He moved slowly along the north coast of Wales and built a road as he went. He used his siege equipment to take Llywellyn's castles one by one and his fleet to bring him his supplies. It also landed English forces on Anglesey during the harvest. This made life very difficult for Llywellyn, who was now cut off from his food supplies. Finally, Llywellyn surrendered and lost all his lands except his own base in Gwynedd.

In 1282 the Welsh, who were determined people, rose up again. This time they were totally crushed. Llywellyn himself was killed. His head was cut off, sent to London and fixed on a spear on one of the gates of the Tower of London. Welsh independence was over, and English rule was established.

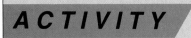

ACTIVITY

Llywellyn and the Welsh

They know the land with its high mountains, dense woods and steep valleys. They have castles at key points. There are few roads. They are close to their own homes and supplies of food, especially grain from Anglesey. They are used to rapid attacks and sudden raids.

Edward and the English

Edward has access to more soldiers than Llywellyn. He has up to 15,000 experienced soldiers. He has the equipment for sieges and attacks on castles and can make use of a fleet of ships. His land forces move very slowly. If he moves into Wales he will be a long way from his supply bases.

How would you advise Edward I to attack Llywellyn of Gwynedd? What strategy would you use?

SOURCE 10

Beaumaris Castle, a concentric castle built by Edward I in the late 13th century.

Castles

Edward built large castles in North Wales, for example, at Conway, Caernarvon, Beaumaris and Harlech. You can see Beaumaris Castle in Source 10. Edward hired Master James of St George, the best castle architect in Europe, to build his castles to the latest designs. Many castles had walled towns attached to them as Source 11 shows.

Small numbers of soldiers could defend these castles against the Welsh if they should rebel again. All the castles could be supplied by sea. This meant they could provide a base for the English if necessary. Most of all, these castles provided a strong deterrent for the Welsh and were symbols of English power.

English government

North Wales was now governed by English officials from Caernarvon Castle, while South Wales was governed from Carmarthen Castle. The Statute of Rhuddlan, which was passed in 1284, laid down the future system of government. Wales was divided into counties and English county officials, such as sheriffs, were appointed to collect taxes from the people. English law became the law of the land. The Welsh were allowed to keep some of their laws and customs, but these did not apply to Englishmen.

Naturally the Welsh people bitterly resented these changes. For example, under Welsh law, if a lord lost his land it was returned to the common people. Under English law it went to the king. They objected to the new English officials who collected their taxes. While English settlers were given land in Wales, the Welsh were excluded from the new towns (see Source 12).

SOURCE 12

Extract from an Ordinance of 1295, showing the restrictions placed on the Welsh by the English.

'The Welsh shall not purchase lands in the English walled boroughs. It was ordained by Lord Edward the conqueror that no Welshman should dwell in the walled towns, but should be removed by the mayors of these towns. No Welshman should make any business arrangements outside the towns, nor should brew beer for sale.'

SOURCE 11
Caernarvon Castle and the walled town of Caernarvon.

1   In what way does the law in Source 12 discriminate against the Welsh, because of their nationality?

2   In what other ways were the Welsh made to feel like second-class citizens in their own country?

Owain Glyndwr

Wales no longer had any princes to lead the country, so over the next 100 years, leadership passed to educated landowners. It was to these people that the bards, the Welsh poets, sang and recited their poems. They told of the terrible defeat that Wales had suffered in 1282, and kept alive the memory of the great deeds of her princes.

One of these landowners was Owain Glyndwr. He had a large house on a fine estate at Sycharth, in North Wales. He had been educated in London and was a friend of the English poet Geoffrey Chaucer. In 1400 he had a dispute over land with another Welsh lord. This lord put his case to the English king, Henry IV, who decided in his favour. Owain Glyndwr was furious. He raised a small force and attacked English towns in North Wales. Within months a national rebellion was under way. Both peasants and landowners joined in the rebellion. Welsh students at Oxford and Cambridge universities rushed home to join the army. Even Welsh monks joined in. The abbot of Llantarnam, for example, fought in several battles. This was not just a rising of a Welsh prince and his followers. This was a national rebellion.

Owain Glyndwr proved to be a brilliant leader. By 1404 almost all of Wales was under his control. The English were divided by civil war, and Glyndwr formed an alliance with the English rebels against King Henry IV. He also had plans for an independent nation of Wales and called a Parliament at Machynlleth (see Source 13). He negotiated with the pope and asked for St David's to become an ARCHBISHOPRIC, free from Canterbury. He also laid plans for two universities to be founded.

However, the revolt gradually subsided. By 1406, Henry IV had won control of England and turned to re-capturing his castles in Wales. The last battle was in 1410. Glyndwr was never captured, but died about 1415. Even though all these events took place over 500 years ago, Owain Glyndwr is still a hero to the Welsh.

SOURCE 13
Owain Glyndwr's parliament house at Machynlleth.

attainment target 1

1 Look at the first part of this section on Wales. Make a list of the changes that the Normans brought to Wales.

2 How much do you think Wales changed in the century after the Norman Conquest?

3 Why would your answer to question 2 be different if you lived at either of the areas marked *A* or *B* in Source 6?

4 Look at Source 6. If you lived at *B*, do you think you would regard the Norman marcher lords as good or bad for your region? What might affect your decision?

5 Describe the changes that Edward I made to the law, government and the towns in Wales after his victory in 1282.

6 How were these changes linked?

7 Both Llywellyn's war of 1282 and Owain Glyndwr's revolt of 1400 were protests against English interference in Wales. In what ways were they different?

8 Draw a timeline of Welsh history to cover the years 1250 to 1400. Mark on it the main dates in this unit.

Scotland

Scotland, at this time, was also a divided land. Each area had its own particular character. The Lowlands were hilly, but were also very fertile (see Source 15).

The Highlands of Scotland formed a separate land and the local kings did not control this area as easily as other parts of Scotland (see Source 16). In fact, until 1266, the Western Isles had belonged to the King of Norway who had ruled there since the Viking invasion.

---

1 What is your impression of Scotland from Sources 15 and 16?

2 In what ways does Scotland seem to be different from England at this time, and in what ways was it the same?

'The country is difficult and hard to travel. To a man on horseback, the hills are impassable, some here and there. The woods are full of deer. The land of the seaboard is fairly level and fertile with green pasture and rich cornland fit for beans, peas and all the crops.'

SOURCE 15
Extract describing the Lowlands of Scotland in the Middle Ages, written by John of Fordun in the 14th century.

In the Highlands the fields are poor, except for oats and barley. The country has ugly stretches of moor and boggy ground. The country is rich in horses and sheep and has a great wealth of fish. The Scots speak two languages. Those who speak Gaelic live in the Highlands and islands. The Highlanders are a savage and untamed people who are primitive and proud. They are fond of plunder and an easy life.

SOURCE 16
This extract, which describes the Highlands of Scotland in the Middle Ages, was written by John of Fordun in the 14th century.

SOURCE 14
Dundrennan Abbey, a 12th century abbey in the lowlands of Scotland.

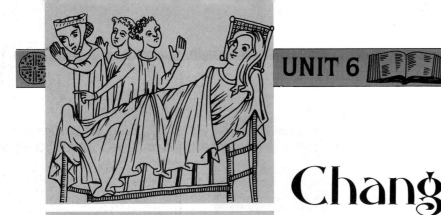

Changing times

In this unit, we will look at two dramatic events from 14th century history, the Black Death and the Peasants' Revolt.

The population of Britain rose slowly but steadily throughout the Middle Ages. Then in 1348 and 1349 over one third of the population died in the Black Death. This unit examines the causes and the consequences of this disaster. We will also find out how some of the consequences of the Black Death helped to cause the Peasants' Revolt.

The Middle Ages was a period of change. Sometimes change happens gradually as in the story of the village of Bawsey, in Norfolk (see Source 1). Bawsey village grew slowly over several generations. Then, after many villagers died in the Black Death of 1348 to 1349, it began to decline. Nevertheless, the decline was slow and a few people still lived there in the 16th century. It was then abandoned completely. The church slowly began to fall down, until it became the ruin you can see in Source 1. The whole story took nearly 1,000 years.

Sources 2 and 3 show much more rapid change. Source 2, for example, describes the arrival of the BLACK DEATH. Between 1348 and 1349, one third of the population of Britain died from this plague both in towns and country. In some towns people died at the rate of 200 a day, and scenes like those we can see in Source 3 happened.

The Black Death, in turn, helped to bring about the Peasants' Revolt of 1381. In Source 4 you can see John Ball who led the peasants' march to London.

SOURCE 1

Abandoned village church at Bawsey in Norfolk.

SOURCE 2

A chronicle describes the arrival of the Black Death in 1348.

In this year 1348 in Melcombe Regis in the County of Dorset, a little before the feast of St John the Baptist, two ships docked. One was from Bristol, the other from France, and one of the sailors brought with him the terrible plague.

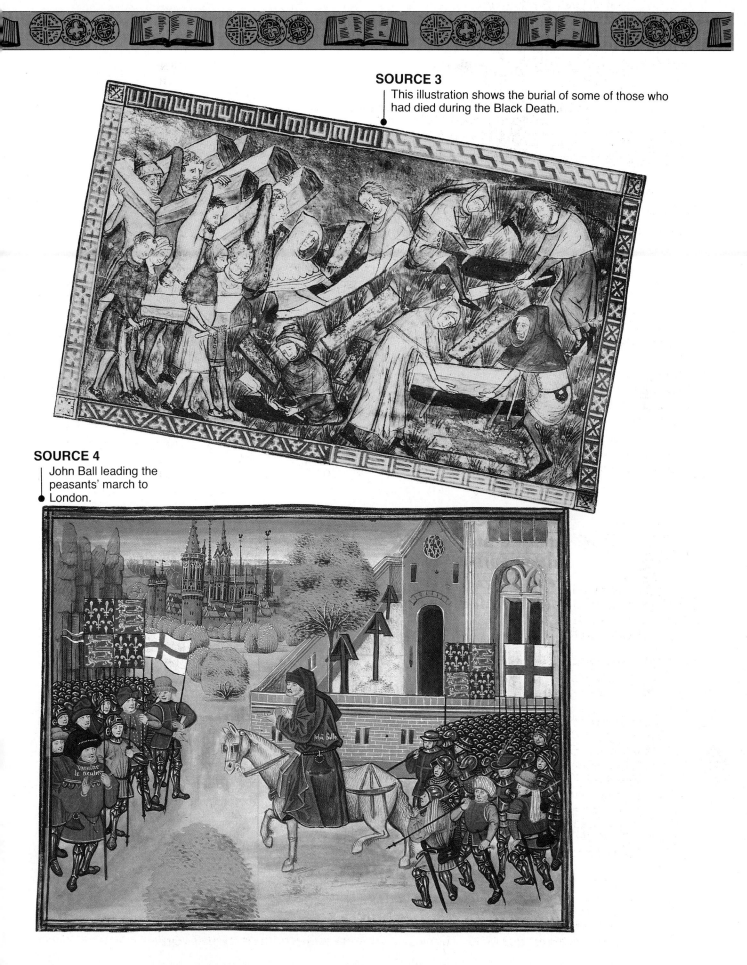

SOURCE 3

This illustration shows the burial of some of those who had died during the Black Death.

SOURCE 4

John Ball leading the peasants' march to London.

Population growth

It is difficult to tell how many people there were in England in the Middle Ages, because the first census was not taken until 1801. However, historians have made rough estimates, using the evidence available. Using the *Domesday Book*, they have estimated the population in 1086 to be about 1.5 million. They worked out that over the next 250 years it rose to about 4.5 or even 5 million. This is obviously an enormous increase, even though it was spread over 250 years. What were the results of this tripling of the number of people in England?

Effect on farming

First of all, of course, these people had to be fed. This meant they had to find more land to farm. Over the centuries the unused land between villages, called waste, was gradually ploughed up, and woods were cut down, as Source 5 shows. Where there was no spare land to be cleared or drained, hillsides were cut into terraces, called lynchets (see Source 6).

'Bishop Roger of Worcester granted some woodland at Bishop's Cleeve to Girold, at a rent of 1 mark (67p) a year. Girold had cleared 170 acres of this wood and added them to the open fields of the village.'

SOURCE 5
This source, by W G Hoskins, describes how woodland was cleared.

Effect on villagers

The diagrams in Source 7 will help you to work out whether prices went up or down in any given situation. Source 7a tells us the price of food at this time of growing population. The *supply* of food increased slightly as more land was farmed, but the *demand* for food increased a lot with three times the number of people to be fed. The *result* was high food prices. Source 7b shows what happened to wages. As the population grew, the *supply* of workers increased. However, the *demand* for workers only increased a little. This *resulted* in low wages.

By the early 14th century life was very difficult for many people in the village. Wages were low, and food prices were high. This meant that many people were permanently hungry. In a bad year

people starved to death. Then came the worst disaster the people of Britain have ever had to face: the Black Death.

What do Sources 5 and 6 tell us about the lives of villagers in the Middle Ages?

SOURCE 6
Lynchets in Somerset. Hillsides were cut into terraces called lynchets.

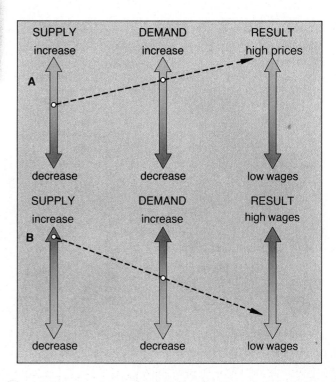

SOURCE 7
Supply and demand for land and labour and effects on wages and prices.

The Black Death

The Black Death was a plague that killed a large number of the population. Sources 8 and 9 describe the symptoms and the results of the plague. The writer of Source 8 describes a 'shilling in the armpit'. This was a lump or boil as big as a 5p piece. The boils oozed pus and blood, then burst. Victims coughed blood and vomited, and smelt badly. They usually died in three or four days. Source 9 shows that the effects of the Black Death were widespread and devastating. No one was spared from the disease. It attacked people in all social groups, rich and poor, young and old. Source 10 shows death as a person. He strikes at all groups of people in a weird dance, which became known as the 'dance of death'.

Scientists now call this disease bubonic plague. This term comes from the boils or lumps described in Source 8, called buboes. In 1894 they discovered that it was caused by bacteria that lived on a type of flea carried by black rats. When the rat died the flea moved to humans and so the bacteria entered the bloodstream.

In Source 10, who does death carry away?

'Woe is me of the shilling in the armpit; it is a white lump that gives pain, a painful angry knob. It is like an apple, like the head of an onion, a small boil that spares no one. Great is its seething, like a burning cinder.'

SOURCE 8
Getlin, a Welsh writer, describes the various symptoms of the Black Death.

'In this year (1349) a plague of a kind which had never been met with before ravaged our land of England. The Bishop of Rochester lost four priests, five squires, ten attendants, seven young clerics and six pages, so that nobody was left to serve him in any capacity. At Malling Abbey he consecrated two abbesses. Both died almost immediately, leaving only four nuns and four novices.'

SOURCE 9
In this source from the *Chronicle of William of Dene* we can see the results of the disease upon the population.

SOURCE 10
The dance of death, in which 'death' carries off its victims in a weird dance.

As we saw in Unit 3, living conditions in Britain in the Middle Ages allowed rats to flourish. Towns were crowded and dirty, which encouraged disease. There were also plenty of rats in the villages: in the thatched roofs and in piles of rubbish in the corners of the earth floors of the villagers' cottages. The real cause of the Black Death was not known at this time. This was one reason why the disease was so frightening.

'Toads should be dried in the sun and they should be laid on the boil. The toad will swell and draw out the poison of the plague to its own body. When it is full it should be thrown away and another toad applied to the boil.'

SOURCE 12

An example of a doctor's advice to some of the plague victims.

SOURCE 11

Flagellant procession. These people travelled about whipping each other. They believed that the Black Death was God's punishment.

'You are to make sure that all the human excrement and other filth lying in the streets of the city is removed. You are to cause the city to be cleared from all bad smells, so that no more people will die from such smells.'

SOURCE 13

An extract from a letter from Edward III to the Lord Mayor of London in 1349. Note that he blames the smells for killing people.

Here are seven ideas that people used either to avoid catching the disease or to treat it.

1 Burn the clothes of victims.

2 Hold flowers, or strong-smelling spices, to cover the mouth when with a plague victim, or even in the street.

3 Join the flagellants (see Source 11). These people believed that the Black Death was God's punishment on the world. They punished themselves by whipping each other in order to win God's forgiveness.

4 Follow the plague motto 'Quick-Far-Late'. This meant to go away quickly, go far away, and not to come back until late.

5 Follow the doctor's advice in Source 12.

6 Clean the streets (see Source 13).

7 Blame it all on foreigners or people of a different religion. In 1348 in Strasbourg 20,000 Jews were killed by the townspeople.

ACTIVITY

1 Copy out and fill in the following table. Put the number of the idea in the correct column.

No use at all	Would help to avoid the plague	Would cure the plague

2 Do you have any ideas in the first column? If they were no use, why did people believe them?

3 Do you have any ideas in the second column? At the time people did not know the cause of the plague. How did they arrive at ideas which were at least of some use to them?

4 What does this exercise tell you about people's attitudes and beliefs in the Middle Ages?

The plague strikes

The Black Death appears to have started in Asia in 1334 and had reached Eastern Europe by 1346. It spread westwards along trade routes to Southern Russia. By late 1347 it had reached Sicily. There were victims in Southern France by the end of 1347 and in Paris by June 1348. Source 14 shows the effects of the Black Death in Southern Italy. In June 1348 the Black Death arrived in England. By the end of 1349, the whole of the British Isles had been affected. Historians estimate that about one third of the population was wiped out. This means at least one million people died.

Over the next 100 years, the bubonic plague came to Britain again several times, although it was not as bad as the first time. The population did not recover to its pre-Black Death level for 200 years. Life was never the same again for the people of Britain.

'Every joy has ceased in the villages. Pleasant sounds are hushed and every note of gladness has stopped. They have become abodes of horror and a wilderness. Fruitful country places, without workers are deserts and abandoned to barrenness.'

SOURCE 15
Bishop Edyngton of Winchester describes the effect of the plague on village life.

SOURCE 16
Deserted village of Hamilton in Leicestershire. Many villages were deserted as a result of the Black Death.

'No one could be found to bury the dead for money or for friendship. In many places great pits were dug and piled deep with huge heaps of the dead. There were many dead throughout the city, who were so thinly covered with earth that the dogs dragged them forth and ate their bodies.'

SOURCE 14
Agnolo of Siena describes reactions to the Black Death.

Results of the Black Death

Nowadays, after a disaster, social workers attend to the survivors. There were, of course, no social workers in 1349. Some people were in a state of shock or went mad. There was no one to enforce law and order. In some places, people took what they wanted from victims' homes. Normal standards of respect for other people broke down.

Towns were affected more than villages. Busy streets were deserted, and shops and houses were empty. There was always a smell of dead bodies. Gradually life returned to normal. The survivors met up to buy and sell their goods. However, only two thirds of the population had survived and trade was quiet and restricted for a long time.

In the villages, streets and houses were also empty (see Source 15). Crops rotted in the fields and weeds flourished. Some animals died through lack of care. Several villages were abandoned. Those people who were left alive moved away to join the survivors of another village. In the Middle Ages farming needed plenty of people to work together, especially at harvest times. Sometimes villagers struggled on for a while, even into the 15th century, before they abandoned their village.

Source 1 and Source 16 both show deserted villages, of which there are thousands in England. Before the Black Death villages had often been started on poor land. These lands were abandoned as people moved back to vacant land in more fertile areas. In Source 16 you can see the deserted village of Hamilton, with the rectangles of the lord's moated house and his fishponds. You can see the village street and some of the villagers' houses. You may also be able to see the strips in the old, open fields. Hamilton was abandoned in the 15th century.

John Ball

John Ball was a poor priest who criticised the rich leaders of the Church. He was not allowed to preach in churches, so he preached to the people wherever they were, in the market place and on the village green. He spoke about Adam and Eve in the Garden of Eden, a story which was very familiar to his listeners (see Source 22). Ball, who preached that there was no need for idle lords, said:

'When Adam delved (dug) and Eve span,
Who was then the gentleman?'

At the beginning of time there were just two people, who worked hard like peasants. There were no gentlemen in the Garden of Eden, who lived on the backs of the poor.

Taxes

Edward III died in 1377. His son, Richard II, was a boy of 10 when he became king. His advisers, Simon of Sudbury, Archbishop of Canterbury, and Sir John Hales, wanted to continue the war with France. For this they needed money, and asked for a poll tax of one groat (4d). In 1379 they asked for another groat, and in 1380 three groats, 12d (5p). Richard II's advisers asked the

SOURCE 22
Adam and Eve in the Garden of Eden.

rich to pay more than the poor, but the people were still furious. Many hid from the tax-collectors, or lied about the number of adults there were in their family. In 1381, the government sent round its officials to check the tax lists. The people thought they were being asked for another 4d and took up their weapons.

The revolt

On 30th May 1381 villagers in Essex attacked royal officials. In early June there were riots in Kent and Lesnes Abbey was attacked. The rebels in these two counties kept in contact with each other. In Kent the rebels freed John Ball from Maidstone prison on 7th June, and made Wat Tyler their leader. In both counties they attacked the houses of tax collectors and lawyers, and burnt the legal records which proved they were villeins. On 11th June, both groups of rebels marched to London. By 12th June there were 60,000 rebels camped outside the city of London (see Source 23). John Ball preached to the Kentish rebels at Blackheath as described in Source 24.

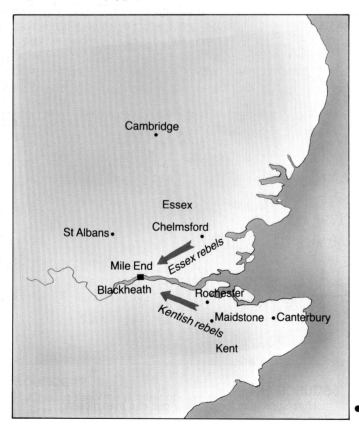

SOURCE 23
Map to show the movement of Kentish and Essex rebels on London.

'My good friends, things cannot go well in England until everyone is equal. Then there shall be neither slaves nor lords, and lords be no more masters than we are. How ill they treat us! Are we not all descended from the same ancestors, Adam and Eve?

They are dressed in velvet and other rich clothes and decorated with ermine, while we are forced to wear rags. They have wines, spices and fine bread, while we have only black bread and scraps from the straw. They have handsome houses, while we must brave the wind and rain to labour in the field. We are called slaves, and if we do not perform our services we are beaten.

We have no one to whom we can complain, who is willing to hear us. Let us go to the king and argue with him. He is young and from him we may get a good answer. If not, we ourselves must try to put things right.'

SOURCE 24

Extract from John Ball's sermon preached to the Kentish rebels at Blackheath, as recorded by the chronicle of Jean Froissart.

1   In Source 24 how did John Ball stir up the anger of the peasants?

2   In Source 24 to whom do the peasants want to appeal?

3   What do they threaten to do if that person doesn't help them?

4   Source 24 is an extract from the writings of a Frenchman, Jean Froissart. He was alive at the time, and may have been in England, but was not at Blackheath. How reliable do you think Source 24 is?

SOURCE 25

The death of Simon of Sudbury and Sir John Hales at the hands of the rebels.

Richard's advisers didn't know what to do. They had no army or police force. They had to talk to the rebels. Richard took a boat from the Tower down river to meet the rebels, but did not land. They shouted to him to land and talk about their problems. Richard refused and hurried back to the Tower. On 13th June the rebels got into London. They attacked the homes of the royal officials whom they blamed for the poll tax. On 14th June 1381 Richard met them outside the city at Mile End. He was prepared to agree to their demands if he could persuade them to return home. Wat Tyler demanded that the king's advisers should be sentenced to death. The peasants blamed them for their problems. Richard agreed to this because he had no choice. Some of the rebels then began to return home, but some peasants took Richard at his word and began to hunt down royal officials. Simon of Sudbury and Sir John Hales were killed (see Source 25). The rebels then went on the rampage in London. Many were drunk, houses were looted and people killed. Wat Tyler's peasant army was beginning to break up.

The death of Wat Tyler

On 15th June Richard II met Wat Tyler at Smithfield. We do not know exactly what happened, but it would appear that Tyler irritated the king's attendants. He may have talked disrespectfully to the king, grabbed the bridle of his horse, or spat on the ground. There was a scuffle, Tyler drew his dagger, but was killed by one of the king's attendants. The rebels began to move forward and it looked as if the royal party would be massacred. Richard II then rode up to the rebels and shouted *'I will be your leader'*. The rebels, always loyal to the king, followed him. Both these incidents can be seen in Source 26.

The end of the revolt

The Mayor of London and his soldiers drove the rest of the rebels out of the city. On the same day other groups of peasants attacked the abbeys at Bury St Edmunds and St Albans. However, with the main rebellion over these other actions petered out. Royal forces rounded up the leaders of the revolt and many were hanged. John Ball was hanged and beheaded at St Albans on 15th July. By autumn 1381 the revolt was all over.

Consequences of the revolt

In the short term the revolt was a total failure. Richard withdrew all his promises. He told Essex peasants at Waltham Cross: *'Villeins you were and villeins you shall remain'*.

In the long term, however, the rebels were victorious. The poll tax was not used again for 600 years. The efforts to keep wages under control never really succeeded. The shortage of workers continued for many years, which gave the peasants the upper hand. Within 100 years all the peasants had won their freedom from labour services. By 1500 there were no villeins.

SOURCE 26

The killing of Wat Tyler, from a 15th century edition of Froissart's Chronicle.

attainment target 1

The Black Death	Statute of Labourers
John Ball's sermons	Poll Tax
French Wars	Wat Tyler

1 Choose three items from this table which you think were important causes of the Peasants' Revolt. Explain each one, saying why you think it was important.

2 Add one other cause of the Peasants' Revolt which is not in this table and explain your choice.

3 Choose one item from this table which was an important short-term cause of the Peasants' Revolt.

4 Choose one item from this table which was an important long-term cause of the Peasants' Revolt.

5 If Parliament had not passed the Statute of Labourers, do you think the Peasants' Revolt would have happened?

ACTIVITY

Market day

This is an activity for the whole class. Half of the class are stall-holders at a market in a medieval town. The other half are customers.

Stall-holders
Here are some trades to choose from. It doesn't matter if more than one person chooses the same trade, but it could mean having to lower your prices to compete with your rivals:

Fishmonger	Shoemaker
Potter	Glover
Spicer	Vintner (sold wine)
Draper	Haberdasher (sold small items like shoelaces, beads, thread, pegs,
Goldsmith	toys)
Butcher	Fletcher
Tailor	Scrivener
Baker	Grocer

Customers
Decide who you are going to be. You could be:
villagers, coming into town to sell milk, eggs, cheese and buy butter or, essential supplies
a rich lord or lady
a burgess, looking for a present for a friend's birthday
an apprentice, looking for a present to take home to your mother
a foreigner, looking for local goods
a priest, doing the daily shopping
a nun, shopping for the rest of the members of your nunnery
the constable, making sure the law is kept

Here are some other things to remember:
Prices would be much lower than they are today. For example:

Fish	best mackerel ½p each
	pickled herrings 1p a pound
	wriggling eels, all fresh 25 for 1p
Cloth:	Velvet £1 an ell (an ell measures from finger tip to the opposite shoulder – about 112 cm)
	Satin 33p an ell
	Linen 20p an ell
Haberdashery:	Two dozen red leather shoelaces 3p
	One string of jet beads 2p

(jet is a shiny black stone)
One green leather purse 2p
Two pounds of thread 10p

1 Stallholders set up your stalls and decide what you want to sell, at what prices. Customers decide what you want to buy. Your teacher will then declare the market open.

2 After a little while an entertainer appears. (Perhaps one member of the class can do handstands, or juggle.) Everyone stops to watch. Someone steals something off a stall. The entertainment ends and everyone gives the entertainer a penny. Then the theft is discovered. The constable has to investigate.

3 One of the customers accuses one of the traders of unfair dealing (short measure, shoddy goods, bad food etc). An argument breaks out. The constable calls both people to the Court of Pie-Powder – the market court. This consists of six stallholders and six customers. They hear both sides, then make a decision.

Here are some of the punishments that were handed out by the market court at Salisbury:

'*John Penrose sold unsound and unwholesome red wine. He was condemned to drink some of the same wine and have the rest poured over his head.*'
'*John Russell sold 37 pigeons all bad. He had to stand in the pillory and have the pigeons burnt underneath.*'

The pillory was a frame with holes to hold the neck and wrists of the criminal. Stocks held criminals' ankles. Both were used by the Court of Pie-Powder.

| **Noises** | The market place would be very noisy, with people shouting their wares and trying to sell things. Many prices would be argued over. |
| **Smells** | Some nice smells: bread, spices, leather. Some nasty smells: the tannery, bad fish, bad meat. |

4 Writing-up. Each person must now write an account of market-day in Imchester. Try to think what people felt about the market in those days, not what we may feel now.

Glossary

Abbot (Abbess)
The head of an abbey, a community of monks (abbot) or nuns (abbess).

Archbishop
The man in charge of Church organisation over a large area, including several bishops. England has only two archbishops, the Archbishops of Canterbury and York.

Bailey
The outer, fenced enclosure of a motte and bailey castle.

Baptism
A religious ceremony which makes someone a Christian.

Bible
The sacred writings of the Christian religion.

Bishop
The man in charge of Church organisation in an area that includes many parishes. The area he controls is called a diocese.

Black Death
A fatal disease carried by rats, which killed one third of the population in the 14th century.

Chaplain
The personal priest of an important organisation or person.

Christendom
That part of the world inhabited largely by Christians. In this book it means Europe, particularly Western Europe.

Chronicle
A record of events.

Civil War
A war between different groups inside the same country.

Confession
The Christian act of declaring your sins to God or to a priest.

Conquest
The act of taking over an area by force, successfully.

Coronation
The ceremony in which a monarch is crowned.

Crusade
A Christian Holy War.

Excommunicated
Cut off from the Church and all its ritual and support.

Feudalism
The system of organisation of English society in the Middle Ages. Land was given to barons by the king. In return they governed the area they had been given and supplied the monarch with soldiers.

Feudum
Land given to barons by the king, which they governed in return.

Government
The system or form by which a community is ruled.

Homage
The act of giving loyalty to your lord.

House of Commons
One of the two chambers of the British Parliament.

Interdict
To exclude a country from the Church.

Invasion
The act of attacking an area or country with armed forces.

Knight
A man who served his lord as an armed mounted soldier.

Labour services
Working for someone without pay as a form of rent for land.

Lollard
A follower of John Wycliffe, during the 14th to 16th centuries.

Magna Carta
The charter granted by King John at Runnymede in 1215.

Manor
An estate of land, usually, but not always, a single village.

Marcher lord
A lord who governs and defends a borderland area.

Middle Ages
Name given to a period of history roughly between the dates of the 5th century AD to AD 1500.

Monarch
Rule by one person – a king or a queen.

Monastery
A religious community of monks, cut off from the world.

Monk
A man who lives in a religious community bound by vows of poverty, chastity and obedience.

Motte
The raised mound which forms part of a motte and bailey castle.

Nave
The central space in a church.

Norman
A person who came from Normandy in France.

Nun/Nunnery
A woman who lives in a religious community called a nunnery, who is bound by vows of poverty, chastity and obedience.

Oath
A solemn promise often made with religious support.

Overlord
A supreme lord or master.

Parish
A small area, usually a village, with its own priest and church.

Parliament
A meeting of representatives of towns and shires.

Peasant
A poor person who lives by working on the land.

Penance
To punish yourself for your sins.

Pilgrim
A person who goes on a journey to a place of special religious importance.

Priest
A person who carries out religious duties and ceremonies.

Prior/Prioress
The head of a community in certain religious orders.

Reeve
The village foreman. A peasant who organised the work of the other peasants.

Roman Catholic
A follower of the Roman Catholic religion, one of the main Christian religions.

Sanctuary
A religious building where people on the run from the law were safe from arrest.

Sheriff
The chief royal official in any county, who was mainly responsible at this time for collecting taxes.

Shire
A county.

Shrine
A place of worship related to a sacred object or person.

Statute
A law that is passed by Parliament.

Tapestry
A picture made by weaving coloured threads into a backing, usually used as a wall-hanging. (Strictly speaking, the Bayeux tapestry is not a tapestry.)

Tax
Money paid to the government.

Tithe
A kind of tax, usually about one tenth of the produce of your land, which you had to pay to the Church.

Vassal
Someone who pays homage to a lord in return for land.

Villein
A peasant who is bound to his lord, for whom he has to do particular services.

Timeline

1050	
1075	1066 : Battle of Hastings 1069 : Harrying of the North
	1086 : *Domesday Book*
1100	1108 : English settle in Pembrokeshire, South Wales
1125	
	1135–1154 : Civil War
1150	1154–1189 : King Henry II
	1166 : Assize of Clarendon
1175	1170 : Murder of Thomas Becket. Strongbow becomes King of Leinster, in Ireland
	1199–1216 : King John
1200	
	1215 : Magna Carta
1225	
1250	
	1265 : Simon de Montfort's Parliament
1275	1277 : Edward I defeats the Welsh 1282 : Death of Llywellyn, last King of Wales 1284 : Statute of Rhuddlan
1300	1306 : Robert Bruce leads Scots against English 1314 : Battle of Bannockburn 1320 : Declaration of Arbroath
1325	
	1337–1453 : Hundred Years War
1350	1348–1349 : Black Death
1375	
	1381 : Peasants' Revolt 1382 : Wycliffe's Bible in English
1400	1400 : Owain Glyndwr's rebellion

Index

First published 1991 by CollinsEducational
77–85 Fulham Palace Road
Hammersmith
London W6 8JB

ISBN 0–00–327233–8

Cover designed by Glynis Edwards
Book designed by Sally Boothroyd
Edited by Lesley Taylor
Series planning by Nicole Lagneau
Picture research by Caroline Thompson
Artwork by John Booth, Peter Dennis and Angela Lumley
Production by Ken Ruskin and Mandy Inness

Typeset by CG Graphic Services, Aylesbury, Bucks

Printed and bound by Stige-Arti Grafiche, Italy

Acknowledgements

Every effort has been made to contact the holders of copyright material but if any have been inadvertently overlooked the publishers will be pleased to make the necessary arrangements at the first opportunity.

Photographs The publishers would like to thank the following for permission to reproduce photographs on these pages.

T = top, B = bottom, R = right, C = centre, L = left

Aerofilms Ltd 32T, 58, 59; Alecto Historical Editions 27; Allsport 54; Ancient Art & Architecture Collection 55T; Mr M F Bennett 24L ; Bibliothèque Nationale, Paris 35T; Bodleian Library, Oxford 25B, 34R, 35C, 41L, 43B, 46C&T, 49BL; Bridgeman Art Library 22; British Library 11R, 18T, 19B, 20, 25T, 29B, 33L&R, 35B, 36CL, 48TR, 52L, 55B, 65B, 72T, 73, 74; The Burrell Collection 17T; Mr P Burton 45C; CADW; Welsh Historic Monuments, Crown Copyright 56R; Committee for Aerial Photography, University of Cambridge 29T, 39CR, 69; The President and Fellows: Corpus Christi College, Oxford 17B; Duke of Roxburghe 62; Edinburgh Photographic Library 61; English Heritage 12B, 53T; Essex County Council Planning Department 50B; Fotomas Index 4R, 5B; Tim Graham Picture Library 14L; Harrogate Resort Services Department 39T; Michael Havindean (from: *The Somerset Landscape*) 66T; Clive Hicks 47T; The Controller of Her Majesty's Stationery Office, Crown Copyright 63B; Hulton Picture Company 21, 51L, 68; John Arthur/Impact Photos 14R; Jarrold Publishing 39CL, 42; The Mansell Collection 53B, 65T, 67; Michael Holford 4, 5, 6T, 8B, 9, 10, 11, 12T; Richard Muir 64; Museum of London 43T; National Library of Scotland 63T; The Pierpont Morgan Library, New York (M638 f27v) 19T; Public Record Office 26; Royal Commission on the Historical Monuments, of England 15, 24R, 44, 48L, 52T; Slide File 57B; Mike Read/ Swift Picture Library 50T; Windsor Castle, Royal Library (c) 1991, Her Majesty the Queen 23; Scala 34L, 48BR; Michael Smith 60; Syndication International Ltd 11T; Caroline Thompson 45T, 46B; Master and Fellows of Trinity College, Cambridge 49T, 71; Universitats Bibliothek, Heidelberg 16B; Janet & Colin Bord/Wales Scene 32B; Weald and Downland Museum, Sussex 31T; Philip Wolmuth 45B; Woodmansterne Picture Library 13.

Cover photograph: Bodleian Library, Oxford.